M000187491

3-Minute
DAILY
BLESSINGS

for Women

Print ISBN 978-1-63609-001-6

Scripture quotations marked AMPC are taken from the Amplified® Bible, Classic Edition © 1954, 1958, 1962, 1964, 1965, 1987 by The Lockman Foundation. Used by permission.

Scripture quotations marked CEV are from the Contemporary English Version, Copyright © 1995 by American Bible Society. Used by permission.

Scripture quotations marked ESV are taken from The Holy Bible, English Standard Version®, copyright © 2001 by Crossway Bibles, a publishing ministry of Good News Publishers. Used by permission. All rights reserved.

Scripture marked GNT taken from the Good News Translation® (Today's English Standard Version, Second Edition), Copyright © 1992 American Bible Society. All rights reserved.

Scripture quotations marked KJV are taken from the King James Version of the Bible.

Scripture quotations marked MSG are from *THE MESSAGE*. Copyright © by Eugene H. Peterson 1993, 1994, 1995, 1996, 2000, 2001, 2002. Used by permission of NavPress Publishing Group.

Scripture quotations marked NASB are taken from the New American Standard Bible (NASB 1995), © 1960, 1962, 1963, 1968, 1971, 1972, 1973, 1975, 1977, 1995 by The Lockman Foundation. Used by permission.

Scripture quotations marked NCV are taken from the New Century Version of the Bible, copyright © 2005 by Thomas Nelson, Inc. Used by permission. All rights reserved.

Scripture quotations marked NIrV are taken from the Holy Bible, NEW INTERNATIONAL READER'S VERSION®. Copyright © 1996, 1998 Biblica. All rights reserved throughout the world. Used by permission of Biblica.

Scripture quotations marked NIV are taken from the HOLY BIBLE, NEW INTERNATIONAL VERSION®. NIV®. Copyright © 1973, 1978, 1984, 2011 by Biblica, Inc.™ Used by permission. All rights reserved worldwide.

Scripture quotations marked NKJV are taken from the New King James Version®. Copyright © 1982 by Thomas Nelson, Inc. Used by permission. All rights reserved.

Scripture quotations marked NLT are taken from the *Holy Bible*. New Living Translation copyright© 1996, 2004, 2015 by Tyndale House Foundation. Used by permission of Tyndale House Publishers, Inc. Carol Stream, Illinois 60188. All rights reserved.

Scripture quotations marked NRSV are taken from the New Revised Standard Version Bible, copyright 1989, Division of Christian Education of the National Council of the Churches of Christ in the United States of America. Used by permission. All rights reserved.

Scripture quotations marked TLB are taken from The Living Bible © 1971. Used by permission of Tyndale House Publishers, Inc. Carol Stream, Illinois 60188. All rights reserved.

Published by Barbour Publishing, Inc., 1810 Barbour Drive, Uhrichsville, Ohio 44683, www.barbourbooks.com

Our mission is to inspire the world with the life-changing message of the Bible.

Member of the
Evangelical Christian
Publishers Association

Printed in China.

EMILY BIGGERS   REBECCA CURRINGTON   JANICE THOMPSON

3-Minute
DAILY
BLESSINGS

❋

for Women

**365
ENCOURAGING
DEVOTIONS**

BARBOUR
PUBLISHING

Day 1

GOD'S GIFT OF ABILITIES

*We have different gifts, according
to the grace given to each of us.*
Romans 12:6 niv

God has blessed every born-again believer—every single one—
with some gift or ability with which to serve others and bring
glory to His name. Some abilities are obvious—they shine
brightly in front of everyone—but others move below the
radar. They include things like the ability to pray effectively,
love the unlovely, and listen attentively. Ask God to open your
eyes to your special abilities. They are God's blessings to you.

*Father God, thank You for my special giftedness. Help me
to recognize it and use it to faithfully serve You. Amen.*

Day 2

STRENGTHEN YOUR GIFTS

Do not neglect your gift. . . . Be diligent in these matters; give yourself wholly to them, so that everyone may see your progress.
1 Timothy 4:14–15 niv

The Bible most often refers to the abilities He gives us as gifts because they are given to be given again. If you have the gift of song, God expects you to strengthen and polish that gift and use it to enrich the lives of others. If you have been given a talent for connecting with children, extend that gift to every child you meet. As you use your gifts to bless others, you will be blessed most of all.

God, please fully develop my gifts, talents, and abilities that I might use them for Your glory. Amen.

Day 3

GOD'S JOY IS YOUR STRENGTH

"The joy of the Lord is your strength."
NEHEMIAH 8:10 NIV

Is it really possible to have joy in your everyday life—even when the kids are crying and the bills are piling up? When you're overwhelmed with work or struggling with emotional problems? Can you truly "rejoice and be glad" in the midst of such trials? Of course you can! Joy is a choice, and it's one the Lord hopes you'll make in every situation. His joy will give you the strength you need to make it through. So rejoice, dear one. Rejoice!

Father, help me to find and focus on the bright spots today. Your mercies are new every morning, and there is always a reason to rejoice.

Day 4

GOD HEALS YOUR ANXIETIES

Search me, God, and know my heart;
test me and know my anxious thoughts.
PSALM 139:23 NIV

Have you ever asked the Lord to give you an "anxiety check"? He longs for you to live in peace, but that won't happen as long as you're driven by worries and fears. Today, allow Him to search your heart. Ask Him to dig deep. Are there cobwebs that need to be swept out? Things hidden that should be revealed? Let God wash away your anxieties, replacing them with His exceeding great joy!

Lord, please renew my faith and turn my anxious
thoughts into peace so wonderful that I'm unable
to explain it. In Jesus' name, amen.

Day 5

BE ANXIETY-FREE

*Be anxious for nothing, but in everything by
prayer and supplication, with thanksgiving,
let your requests be made known to God.*
Philippians 4:6 nkjv

Be anxious for nothing? Is that possible? Aren't my anxieties
tied to my emotions? And aren't my emotions tied to the things
that happen to me? I can't control what happens to me, so how
can I control my reactions? Deep breath, friend! Instead of
knee-jerking when troubles come, slip into the throne room
and spend some time giving those problems to the Lord. With
thanksgiving, let your requests be made known to Him.

*Before I react emotionally, Father, remind me to
turn to You in prayer. I cast all my worries on
You because I know You care for me.*

Day 6

GOD'S LOVE
HAS NO LIMITS

*Rejoice in the LORD your God, for he has given you
the autumn rains because he is faithful. He sends you
abundant showers, both autumn and spring rains.*
JOEL 2:23 NIV

As human beings, we are limited in what we can provide for
those we love—our resources, both material and emotional,
are finite. But God has no limits. He blesses His children far
beyond our comprehension. He does more than just rain down
His blessings on us; He sends abundant showers of blessing
in every season of our lives. You are a rich woman. Once you
see all that God has provided for you, you won't ever want to
come in out of the rain.

*Lord, Your blessings never cease to amaze me. Help me
to be aware of them in every season of my life. Amen.*

Day 7

GOD'S LOVE OVERFLOWS

Grace and peace be yours in abundance.
1 PETER 1:2 NIV

As you look around at God's blessings in your life, close your eyes and look inward as well. God has also provided you with an abundance of grace and peace. Grace that allows you to be who you genuinely are and the peace of knowing that who you are is just fine with Him. Women are wonderfully emotional people, the keepers of the inner life. If your inner places are dark and empty, invite God to fill them to overflowing with His goodness.

Lord, I thank You for Your grace and for true peace, which can only be found through Your Son, Jesus, the Messiah. Amen.

Day 8

SPREAD JOY TO FEEL JOY

A miserable heart means a miserable life;
a cheerful heart fills the day with song.
PROVERBS 15:15 MSG

Have you ever felt weighted down? Heavy? Sometimes the cares of this life can make us so anxious that we only see the tips of our toes, not the road ahead. Today, lift your eyes! Speak words of faith and hope over your situation. Go out of your way to cheer someone else up. This simple act will lift your spirits and cause you to forget about your own burdens. Watch the joy sweep in!

God, You are my reason to sing. Renew the song
within my heart today, I ask. In Jesus' name, amen.

Day 9

THOU SHALT NOT WORRY

"Do not worry about tomorrow, for tomorrow will worry about itself. Each day has enough trouble of its own."
MATTHEW 6:34 NIV

What if the Lord had written an eleventh commandment: "Thou shalt not worry"? In a sense, He did! He commands us in various scriptures not to fret. So cast your anxieties on the Lord. Give them up! Let them go! Don't let worries zap your strength and your joy. Today is a gift from the Lord. Don't sacrifice it to fears and frustrations! Let them go and watch God work!

Father, please lighten the concerns that are weighing on my heart today. Remind me that You are in control. Amen.

Day 10

WORK, DON'T WORRY

What do people get for all the toil and anxious striving with which they labor under the sun?
ECCLESIASTES 2:22 NIV

Sometimes, out of anxiety, we bury ourselves in work. We labor from sunup till sundown. There's nothing wrong with working hard, but striving is another thing altogether. When we "strive," we're not trusting God to do His part. We're taking matters into our own hands. Today, take a moment to ask yourself an important question: "Am I working, or am I striving?" Don't let the enemy steal your joy! Strive no more!

God, may I learn day by day to trust You even more. Help me surrender complete control to You. Amen.

Day 11

GARMENTS OF PRAISE

Awake, awake; put on thy strength,
O Zion; put on thy beautiful garments.
ISAIAH 52:1 KJV

Imagine you've been invited to a grand celebration—perhaps a wedding or a banquet. The clothes in your closet are old. Boring. You need a new outfit, one worthy of such an occasion. After serious shopping, you find the perfect dress! It's exquisite, and when you wear it you're in a party frame of mind. That's what God desires from each of us—to "dress" ourselves in garments of praise. It's time to party!

Lord, I praise You, for You are worthy! I want
to bring You honor all my days. Amen.

Day 12

JOY IN THE FACE OF BETRAYAL

Then my head will be exalted above the enemies who surround me; at his sacred tent I will sacrifice with shouts of joy; I will sing and make music to the LORD.

PSALM 27:6 NIV

It's one thing to offer a sacrifice of joy when things are going your way and people are treating you fairly. But when you've been through a terrible betrayal, it's often hard to recapture that feeling of joy. As you face hurts and betrayals, remember that God is the lifter of your head. Sing praises and continue to offer a sacrifice of joy!

Father, I praise You with as much joy and thanksgiving in life's valleys as I do on life's mountaintops. Amen.

Day 13

GOD'S ACCEPTANCE

*[God] chose us in Him before the foundation of the
world. . .according to the good pleasure of His
will, to the praise of the glory of His grace,
by which He made us accepted in the Beloved.*
EPHESIANS 1:4–6 NKJV

You may never receive the full acceptance and approval of
the people in your life. But God has already given you His approval, His acceptance. He chose you. Think about that.
Almighty God chose you! No one compelled Him to. His motive wasn't pity. The Bible says He created you and pronounced
His work "good." He is proud of the "you" He has made, and
He is moved with love for you—just as you are.

*Thank You, heavenly Father, for creating me and for loving
me just as I am. Your stamp of approval means everything.*

Day 14

PRAISE THROUGH SONG

I will praise the name of God with a song,
and will magnify Him with thanksgiving.
PSALM 69:30 NKJV

It's one thing to spend time with God; it's another to praise Him with a thankful heart. Sometimes we forget His many blessings. We praise out of routine. Today, allow God to remind you of all the many ways He has blessed you. Oh, what full and thankful hearts we have when we pause to remember. Now, watch your praises rise to the surface, like cream to the top of the pitcher.

Lord, I pause to count my many blessings today. Thank You for all You do for me, and even more, thank You for who You are.

Day 15

HAPPY ENDURANCE

Behold, we count them happy which endure. Ye have heard
of the patience of Job, and have seen the end of the Lord;
that the Lord is very pitiful, and of tender mercy.
JAMES 5:11 KJV

It's interesting to think of the words *happy* and *endure* in the same sentence. Twenty-first-century Christians are accustomed to a fast-paced life, used to getting what they want when they want it. But sometimes patience is required, especially when we're not feeling well. Want to know the secret of surviving the seasons that try your patience, the ones that wear you to a frazzle? Endure! Happiness will prevail!

Help me to endure the hardest of days, Father God.
Give me the strength I need. Amen.

Day 16

A SEASON OF JOY

Anxiety weighs down the heart, but a kind word cheers it up.
PROVERBS 12:25 NIV

Want to know how to get beyond a season of heaviness? Want to enter a season of joy? Speak uplifting, positive words. The things that come out of your mouth can make or break you. After all, we tend to believe what we hear. So let words of joy flow. Speak hope. Speak life. And watch that spirit of heaviness take flight!

May the words I speak be pleasing to You, Lord. I ask You to renew my joy and fill my heart with Your peace. Amen.

Day 17

ACCEPT OTHERS

Honor God by accepting each other, as Christ has accepted you.
ROMANS 15:7 CEV

Just as God has accepted you, He asks that you accept others. That doesn't mean you must accept their aberrant behaviors or keep your mouth shut when you see people doing things they shouldn't. Accepting others means appreciating that each person was created by and is loved by God. They have value for that reason. In loving Him, you must love whom He loves and accept whom He accepts. That's the only proper response to so great a Creator.

It is You who has made us, Lord. Help me to dwell on this thought today and to find value in each person I meet. Amen.

Day 18

FORGIVING OTHERS

"If you forgive the sins of any, their sins have been forgiven them; if you retain the sins of any, they have been retained."
JOHN 20:23 NASB

Ever known someone who simply refused to forgive? It's one thing to cling to past hurts because you're unable to let go; it's another to do so out of spite. There are no stipulations on forgiveness. We must forgive, regardless of what has been done to us. If you are struggling to release someone who's hurt you, ask the Lord to help you. A miracle of joy will take place as you release your grip.

Lord, help me to forgive those who have hurt me deeply. I know that there will be blessing in the letting go. Amen.

Day 19

ACCOMPLISHING GOD'S WILL

A longing fulfilled is a tree of life.
PROVERBS 13:12 NIV

You are a fortunate woman! You live in a time when women can accomplish anything they set their minds to do. Are there still obstacles? Of course, but nothing you can't deal with. God has given you something special to do in this world. You'll know it by the longing you feel deep inside. Ask God to guide you, lending you His wisdom, grace, and strength. Then go for it. Nothing can compare with the joy of accomplishing God's will for your life.

*Father, thank You for the promptings I sense
from Your Holy Spirit. Show me the way to go,
and I will follow. I desire to do Your will.*

Day 20

REFUGE FROM BETRAYAL

But let all who take refuge in you be glad; let them ever
sing for joy. Spread your protection over them, that
those who love your name may rejoice in you.
Psalm 5:11 niv

Oh, the pain of betrayal. If you've been hurt by someone you trusted, choose to release that person today. Let it go. God is your defender. He has your back. Take refuge in Him. And remember, praising Him—even in the storm—will shift your focus back to where it belongs. Praise the Lord! He is our defense!

Lord Jesus, You are my hiding place, my refuge
in times of trouble. You are my defender,
and I praise Your holy name. Amen.

Day 21

CALL ON GOD FOR HELP

Commit your work to the LORD,
and your plans will be established.
PROVERBS 16:3 ESV

Whatever God has called you to accomplish in your life, He has not called you to accomplish alone. He is always there, providing you with the resources you need to get the job done. That doesn't mean you won't stumble along the way or encounter difficulties. But it does mean that you can call upon the counsel and resources of almighty God to help you. Whether you need wisdom, inspiration, confidence, strength, or just plain tenacity, you will find your answer in Him.

Lord, today I commit myself to You. Help me to work as
though I'm working for You and no one else.
May my work bring You glory. Amen.

Day 22

REJOICE IN HOPE

[Be] rejoicing in hope; patient in tribulation;
continuing steadfastly in prayer.
ROMANS 12:12 NKJV

The words *rejoice* and *hope* just seem to go together, don't they? There's something about choosing joy that fills our hearts with hope for better days ahead. So what if we have to wait awhile? If we stay focused on the Lord, casting our cares on Him, that day of rejoicing will surely come!

God, may I find joy even in the waiting. I know You will teach
me in these hard times. Please grow my faith. Amen.

Day 23

AN ATTITUDE OF JOY

Serve the LORD with gladness; come
before His presence with singing.
PSALM 100:2 NKJV

Attitude is everything. Our attitude determines our outcome. We are challenged by scripture to serve with gladness. (It's funny to think of service and gladness in the same sentence, isn't it?) But here's the truth: if we serve with an attitude of joy, it changes everything. Our service doesn't feel like service anymore. It's a privilege!

Lord, serving really is a lot of fun. I lose myself in it
and forget about my momentary troubles
when I am helping others in Your name.

Day 24
GODLY AMBITION

*Stand firm. Let nothing move you. Always give yourselves
fully to the work of the Lord, because you know
that your labor in the Lord is not in vain.*
1 Corinthians 15:58 niv

Simply defined, ambition means determination to succeed.
That's a positive thing—essential, in fact, to accomplishing
God's will and purpose for your life. It helps you look past the
obstacles in your path—age, health, education, lack of finances,
and so on—to the prize waiting on the other side. God wants
you to be determined, even ambitious. He has given you that
inner motivation to help you complete the task He has assigned
to you. Thank Him for it!

*God, thank You for giving me the ability to work hard and
accomplish the tasks You have set before me. Amen.*

Day 25

PATIENCE FOR MIRACLES

Moses spoke to the people: "Don't be afraid. Stand firm and watch GOD do his work of salvation for you today."
EXODUS 14:13 MSG

When we're waiting on a miracle, the minutes seem to drag by. We force our attention ahead to tomorrow with the hope that we will receive the answer we long for. But what about today? This is the day the Lord has made! He wants us to rejoice in it. So what if the answer hasn't come yet? So what if patience is required? Don't miss the opportunity to connect with God today!

Lord, may my feet be planted firmly in the joy of my salvation as I wait on Your perfect timing. In Jesus' name, amen.

Day 26

DIFFICULT FORGIVENESS

Then Peter came to him and asked, "Lord, how often should I forgive someone who sins against me? Seven times?" "No, not seven times," Jesus replied, "but seventy times seven!"
MATTHEW 18:21–22 NLT

It's easy to get fed up with people who repeatedly hurt you and then ask for forgiveness. We grow weary with their promise that they won't do it again. If someone has repeatedly hurt you, ask the Lord to give you wisdom regarding the relationship, then ask Him to give you the capacity to forgive, even when it seems impossible. Surely joy will rise up in your soul as you watch God at work.

Lord, I am so thankful that there is no limit to Your forgiveness. Give me the grace I need to be more forgiving toward others. Amen.

Day 27

HUMILITY BEFORE GOD

Do nothing out of selfish ambition or vain conceit.
Rather, in humility value others above yourselves.
PHILIPPIANS 2:3 NIV

Ambition is a positive characteristic—unless it begins to take over your life. Are you pursuing your goals—even God-given goals—at the expense of others? Out of control, ambition can cause you to do things you would never do otherwise. God expects you to couple your ambition with godliness. Only then will you truly be accomplishing His will for you. Only then will you truly fulfill the desires He has placed in your heart.

Lord, I confess I often work just for the sake of working.
I begin to believe I can do everything in my
own strength. Humble my heart, please.

Day 28

THIEVES OF JOY

"The thief comes only to steal and kill and destroy; I have come that they may have life, and have it to the full."
JOHN 10:10 NIV

Have you ever been the victim of a robbery? It's a terrible feeling, isn't it? Who would stoop so low? The enemy of your soul is the ultimate thief. His goal? To steal from you. What is he most interested in? Your peace of mind. Your joy. He often uses betrayal as a mode of operation, so be wary! Next time someone hurts you—or betrays you—don't let him or her steal your joy. Stand firm!

Lord, even when people betray me, I know You never will. May I find my joy and peace in You alone. Amen.

Day 29

WAITING SEASONS

But if we hope for that we see not,
then do we with patience wait for it.
ROMANS 8:25 KJV

Are you in a "waiting" season? Is your patience being tested to the breaking point? Take heart! You are not alone. Every godly man and woman from biblical times till now went through seasons of waiting on the Lord. Their secret? They hoped for what they could not see. (They never lost their hope!) And they waited patiently. So, as you're waiting, reflect on the biblical giants and realize you're not alone!

Lord, I can't see what You're doing in my life. And I
certainly don't always understand. Help me to
trust in what I'm unable to see. Grow my faith.

Day 30

THE NECESSITY OF REST

*Therefore my heart is glad and my glory
[my inner self] rejoices; my body too shall
rest and confidently dwell in safety.*

PSALM 16:9 AMPC

Ever wish you could take a day off? Feel like you're always running full-steam ahead? The Lord designed our bodies to require rest, and if we skip that part of the equation, we suffer the consequences! If you want your body to "confidently dwell in safety," then you must get the rest you need. Rest makes for a happy heart—and a healthy body.

*God, as I carve out time to rest this week, I ask You to
bless this time and make it sweet as I quiet
my heart in fellowship with You. Amen.*

Day 31

BEAUTY IS MORE THAN SKIN DEEP

What matters is not your outer appearance—the styling of your hair, the jewelry you wear, the cut of your clothes— but your inner disposition. Cultivate inner beauty, the gentle, gracious kind that God delights in.
1 PETER 3:3–4 MSG

Most women care how they look. That's why they carry mirrors in their purses and purchase billions of dollars of makeup each year. There's nothing wrong with looking good on the outside as long as you remember to primp and preen your inner self as well. God wants your beauty to be more than skin deep. He wants it to be heart deep. Work to be as fully beautiful as you were created to be.

Heavenly Father, please cause me to focus more on the inner me than the outer me. May my acts of kindness reflect Your beauty. Amen.

Day 32

RISE UP

Shout for joy to the LORD, all the earth,
burst into jubilant song with music.
PSALM 98:4 NIV

Do you ever feel like you don't have enough words to praise God? Like your vocabulary is limited? Wish you could throw the lid off and worship Him with abandon? That's exactly what He longs for you to do—spend intimate time with Him. Sing a big song to the Lord. And prepare yourself for the inevitable joy that will rise up as you do.

Lord, I praise You for who You are and not just what
You have done. You are the King of kings and
Lord of lords. I will worship You all my days.

Day 33

FULLNESS OF JOY

And the disciples were filled with joy,
and with the Holy Ghost.
ACTS 13:52 KJV

Want to know the secret of walking in the fullness of joy?
Draw near to the Lord. Allow His Spirit to fill you daily. Let
Him whisper sweet nothings in your ear and woo you with
His love. The Spirit of God is your Comforter, your Friend. He
fills you to overflowing. Watch the joy flow!

Lord, I am blessed to have Your Holy Spirit
guiding and comforting me. May my life
overflow with joy found only in You.

Day 34

LOOKING AHEAD

Let us hold unswervingly to the hope we profess,
for he who promised is faithful.
HEBREWS 10:23 NIV

Change usually shakes us to the core. However, if you've been in a season of great suffering and you sense change is coming, you have reason to celebrate! The sands are shifting. The mourning is coming to an end. God, in His remarkable way, is reaching down with His fingertip and writing, "Look forward to tomorrow!" in the sand. Let the joy of that promise dwell in your heart and bring you peace.

Lord, make my heart steadfast. Help me to
keep my eyes on the path straight ahead.

Day 35

THE PLEASANT SCENT OF FRIENDSHIP

*The sweet smell of perfume and oils is pleasant,
and so is good advice from a friend.*
PROVERBS 27:9 NCV

Friendship is a wonderful gift from God. A good friend leaves behind a "pleasant scent." And when you find a friend who offers wise counsel, you are doubly blessed! Today, don't just seek to find a friend like that; seek to be a friend like that. Leave behind a pleasant aroma to those whom God has placed in your life.

*Lord, thank You for the friends You've placed
in my life. May I be a good friend to others
as well. In Jesus' name I pray. Amen.*

Day 36

LETTING GO OF PAIN

These things have I spoken unto you, that my joy might remain in you, and that your joy might be full.
JOHN 15:11 KJV

When you've been badly hurt, it's hard to let go of the pain, isn't it? Sometimes it can crowd out everything—your peace of mind, your enthusiasm, your joy. If you're struggling with the effects of a betrayal today, don't allow it to consume you. Release it to God. Ask Him to replace the pain with His joy—a joy that will remain in you, never to be stolen again.

God, happiness comes and goes, but the joy I've found in salvation through Your Son is lasting. Thank You for this type of joy. Amen.

Day 37

LOOKING AT THE HEART

*"The LORD does not look at the things people look at.
People look at the outward appearance,
but the LORD looks at the heart."*
1 SAMUEL 16:7 NIV

When God looks at you, He sees a beautiful woman, a temple worthy of His Spirit. He sees your virtuous life and your godly attitudes. He sees a person whose heart has been washed clean and fully submitted to His will and purpose. He sees a beauty that is often missed by others. He sees an inner beauty that transcends any physical characteristics—good or bad. God sees you as you really are.

*Lord, I know You value me. You created me. Please cleanse
and renew my heart that I might live for You.*

Day 38

CHILDREN OF THE MOST HIGH GOD

Yes, joyful are those who live like this! Joyful indeed are those whose God is the LORD.
PSALM 144:15 NLT

How wonderful to realize you're God's child. He loves you and wants nothing but good for you. Doesn't knowing you're His daughter send waves of joy through your soul? How happy we are when we recognize that we are princesses—children of the Most High! Listen closely as He whispers royal secrets in your ear. Your heavenly Father offers you keys to the kingdom and vision for the road ahead.

God, I never quite see myself as a princess. But I'm so glad You do! I'm thankful to be Your daughter and to know the joy of being Yours.

Day 39

A BOOST WHEN YOU'RE DOWN

*David also ordered the Levite leaders to appoint a choir of
Levites who were singers and musicians to sing joyful songs
to the accompaniment of harps, lyres, and cymbals.*
1 CHRONICLES 15:16 NLT

It's tough to lift up your voice when you're feeling down. Sometimes you just don't feel like praising. However, coming together
as a team—a group—somehow boosts your strength. Once
those instruments begin to play and the first few words of the
songs are sung, you're suddenly energized as never before. So
lift your voice with joy in the sanctuary!

*Lord, may I never grow weary of singing Your praises. May
You be honored and lifted up through my worship. Amen.*

Day 40

THE ARMOR OF GOD

*Put on the full armor of God so that you can
take your stand against the devil's schemes.*
Ephesians 6:11 niv

Taking a basic class in self-defense to protect herself in this predator-filled world is a good idea for every woman. A wise woman will learn how to defend herself spiritually as well. God has provided you with a full suit of armor for that purpose—truth, righteousness, peace, faith, and salvation. Wear that suit everywhere you go. You do have an enemy, and he wants to take all you have. Be prepared to resist and defeat him.

*God, as I go into the world, suit me up in Your armor. I will
resist the devil in the powerful name of Jesus, my Savior. Amen.*

Day 41

TRUSTING GOD'S FUTURE FOR YOU

Where there is no vision, the people perish:
but he that keepeth the law, happy is he.
PROVERBS 29:18 KJV

Ever wish you could see into tomorrow? Wish you knew what was coming around the bend? While we can't see into the future, we can prepare for it by trusting God to bring us His very best. And while our "literal" vision can't glimpse the unseen tomorrow, we can prepare for it by staying close to the Lord and spending time in His Word. Peace and joy come when we trust God with our future!

Lord, I don't know what the future holds, but I'm so thankful
to know the One who holds it in His hands. Amen.

Day 42

HEARING GOD'S VOICE

*Blessed is the people that know the joyful sound: they
shall walk, O Lord, in the light of thy countenance.*
Psalm 89:15 kjv

Imagine a dimly lit room. You can barely make out the shapes
of things around you. Somewhere in that room, your Father is
waiting for you. Suddenly His voice rings out and joyous relief
floods your soul. Even though you cannot see where you are
going, the sound of His voice guides you directly into His arms.
Allow yourself to tune in to that precious voice today.

*Lord, when I'm in darkness, remind me of all
You have taught me in the light. Amen.*

Day 43

SINGING THROUGH AFFLICTION

Is any among you afflicted? let him pray.
Is any merry? let him sing psalms.
JAMES 5:13 KJV

It's tough to praise when you're not feeling well, isn't it? But that is exactly what God calls us to do. If you're struggling today, reach way down deep. Out of your pain, your weakness, offer God a sacrifice of praise. Spend serious time in prayer. Lift up a song of joy—even if it's a weak song! You'll be surprised how He energizes you with His great joy!

God, I bring my worries and troubles to You today. I lay them at Your feet. I praise You even in my pain. I know You are the only way to healing.

Day 44

GOD'S WARRIORS

*Our struggle is not against flesh and blood, but against
the rulers, against the authorities, against the powers
of this dark world and against the spiritual
forces of evil in the heavenly realms.*

Ephesians 6:12 niv

In God's kingdom, women are called to be warriors. Alongside
their Christian brothers, they are asked to battle with the forces
of evil that plot to destroy human lives and keep them from
knowing their Creator. This is a warfare fought in the spiritual
realm with an enemy we know is there but whom we cannot
see. Put on your spiritual armor and ask God to point out your
battle station. And then—on to victory!

*God, I'm thankful that I'm fighting in the right army.
May the darkness be overcome by Your light. Amen.*

Day 45

LET PRAYER ROCK YOUR WORLD

But the angel said to him, "Do not be afraid, Zacharias, for your prayer is heard; and your wife Elizabeth will bear you a son, and you shall call his name John."
LUKE 1:13 NKJV

Zacharias, though quite old, had been praying for a child for years. How funny that the angel prepared him by saying, "Don't be afraid," before sharing the news! This answered prayer, though joyous, surely rocked Zacharias and Elizabeth's world! Have you ever consistently prayed for something without getting the answer you want? Ever felt like giving up? Don't! When you least expect it, your answer could come—and it just might rock your world!

Lord, may I hold loosely to my own dreams that I might embrace Your perfect dreams for my life. Amen.

Day 46

SHARING JOY

Tell this news with shouts of joy to the people;
spread it everywhere on earth.
Isaiah 48:20 ncv

Joy is meant to be shared. (It's hard to keep to yourself, after all!) Think of it like a tasty apple pie. You can't eat the whole thing, can you? No, you need to spread the love, share the slices. So it is with joy. When you're going through a particularly joyful season, pass the plates. Sharing is half the fun!

Lord, in my times of rejoicing, remind me to look around
and see those who could use a dose of happiness.
Help me to spread joy wherever I go.

Day 47

YOU ARE ENOUGH

When my skin sags and my bones get brittle,
GOD is rock-firm and faithful.
PSALM 73:26 MSG

It's the nature of a woman to need assurance—confirmation that she is pretty enough, smart enough, pleasing enough. God wants you to know that "you are more than enough." He is pleased with you. He wants you to be assured that He will always be there for you. You need not fear that He will grow tired of you, lose interest, and abandon you. You are precious to Him, no matter your age, your condition, your circumstances. You matter to Him.

Lord, at times I feel so small and insignificant. Show me
today that I am enough and that through You, I can
accomplish great things for Your kingdom.

Day 48

TRUE SATISFACTION

Satisfy us in the morning with your unfailing love,
that we may sing for joy and be glad all our days.
PSALM 90:14 NIV

You've heard the adage, "You're only as old as you feel." One thing that ages us too quickly is discouragement. We get down, and it's hard to get back up again. We need to make a conscious effort each morning to reach out to God and ask Him to satisfy us with His mercy, His loving-kindness. If we're truly satisfied, joy will come. And joy is the best anti-wrinkle cream on the market.

Lord, I find contentment and deep satisfaction in Your love.
May each new day be filled with Your mercies.

Day 49

APPROVED FOR THE KINGDOM

God affirms us, making us a sure thing in Christ, putting his Yes within us. By his Spirit he has stamped us with his eternal pledge—a sure beginning of what he is destined to complete.
2 Corinthians 1:21–22 msg

The last time you bought a house or a car or applied for a loan, were you preapproved? Good feeling, isn't it? In a real sense, you have been preapproved for God's kingdom. He has given you His Word and stamped you with His eternal pledge. You belong to Him. He is fully committed to helping you become all you were created to be. You can turn your back on Him—it's true. But He will never turn His back on you.

Lord, I'm thankful that I'm sealed with the Holy Spirit and fully Yours. Thank You for Your eternal faithfulness. Amen.

Day 50

RENEWING YOUR ATTITUDE

Be constantly renewed in the spirit of your mind
[having a fresh mental and spiritual attitude].
EPHESIANS 4:23 AMPC

Your attitude can substantially affect your happiness level. It's true. When your mind is assaulted every day by "stinkin' thinkin' "—things like "I'm not good enough," "I'm not loved," "I'll never reach my dreams"—it's pretty tough to be happy. On the other hand, when you think about good things—God things—your happiness level will soar. Try it! "God loves me," "God is always by my side, watching out for me," "God has made me a winner." What a difference it will make.

Renew my mind today, heavenly Father, so that I might
dwell on truth rather than lies. You are all I need. Amen.

Day 51

MEANINGFUL PRAYER

*In every prayer of mine I always make my entreaty
and petition for you all with joy (delight).*
PHILIPPIANS 1:4 AMPC

Sometimes we approach our prayer time with God with a list
in hand, much like a child at Christmastime. Other times we
approach the Lord with fear leading the way. "What happens
if He doesn't respond like I hope?" Though we don't need to
come with a Christmas list in hand, we do need to confidently
approach our heavenly Father and make our requests with joy.
He loves us, after all! So draw near!

*Lord, I come before You and thank You for my family and
friends. I pray for their protection, peace, and strength. Amen.*

Day 52

DYING TO YOUR OLD SELF

Put off your old self, which is being corrupted by its deceitful desires; to be made new in the attitude of your minds; and to put on the new self, created to be like God in true righteousness and holiness.
Ephesians 4:22–24 niv

The key to a great attitude is to rise above your old ways of thinking and start thinking like God thinks. The Bible says we aren't capable of thinking God's actual thoughts. They are too high and holy. But you can think like God—raising your mind-sight to focus on the good, the right, the holy, helping and encouraging others, ways to express your thankfulness. An attitude is simply a response to what you see—keep your mind tuned in to the good.

God, help me to remember that my old self has died and that my new self is more than capable, through Christ, of rising above worldly ways of thinking.

Day 53

FRESH WATER

Can both fresh water and salt water
flow from the same spring?
JAMES 3:11 NIV

Can you feel it—that bubbling in your midsection? Can you sense it rising to the surface? Joy comes from the deepest place inside of us, so deep that we often forget it's there at all. Wonder of wonders! It rises up, up, up to the surface and the most delightful thing happens. Troubles vanish. Sorrows disappear. Godly joy has the power to squelch negative emotions. So let the bubbling begin!

Lord, replace my troubles and sorrows with joy
and peace, I pray. In Jesus' name, amen.

Day 54

DILIGENTLY SEEKING GOD

He that cometh to God must believe that he is, and that
he is a rewarder of them that diligently seek him.
HEBREWS 11:6 KJV

Belief is one of those things you can't see physically, but you still have it. For example, you believe a chair will hold you when you sit in it. You can't explain the physics of it, but you sit in it believing it will do what it's supposed to do. Belief in God is like that. You put your trust in Him that He will do what He said He would do. The Bible, His written Word, is filled with those promises.

God, help me to diligently seek You all the days of my life,
rather than being only a Sunday morning Christian
who is too busy throughout the week.

Day 55

SPIRITUAL EXERCISE

A cheerful disposition is good for your health;
gloom and doom leave you bone-tired.
PROVERBS 17:22 MSG

Want to stay in the best possible health? Do you take vitamins every day? Eat right? Exercise? Here's one more thing you can add to your daily regimen for good health—a prescription for long life: cheerfulness. Yes, that's right! To ward off disease, try joy. According to Proverbs 17:22, it's the very flower of health. And it's just what the doctor ordered.

May my life be a reflection of the joy I have in You, Lord.
Replace every complaint with a cheerful word, I pray. Amen.

Day 56

SHOW YOURSELF FRIENDLY

*A man that hath friends must shew himself friendly:
and there is a friend that sticketh closer than a brother.*
PROVERBS 18:24 KJV

Ever met someone who seems to have the gift of friendship?
She's a joy to be around and is always there when you need
her. Perhaps you're that kind of friend to others. Friendship is
a privilege, and we're blessed to have brothers and sisters in
Christ. But not all friendships are easy. Today, ask the Lord to
show you how to "show yourself friendly" in every situation.
Oh, the joy of great relationships!

*Lord, help me to be a true friend to those around me. May my
kindness reflect the compassion that You have shown me. Amen.*

Day 57

THIS TOO
SHALL PASS

But even if you should suffer for what is right, you are blessed. "Do not fear their threats; do not be frightened."
1 Peter 3:14 niv

It's one thing to suffer because of something you've done wrong; it's another to suffer for doing right. Even when we're unjustly persecuted, God wants us to respond in the right way. If you're suffering as a result of something you've done for the Lord, be happy! Keep a stiff upper lip! This too shall pass, and you can come through it with a joyful attitude.

Lord, You suffered greatly on my behalf, and You had done nothing wrong. Help me to respond with grace when I face suffering of any kind.

Day 58

QUENCHING YOUR SPIRITUAL THIRST

On the last and greatest day of the festival, Jesus stood and said in a loud voice, "Let anyone who is thirsty come to me and drink. Whoever believes in me, as the Scripture has said, rivers of living water will flow from within them."
JOHN 7:37–38 NIV

Ever been so thirsty that nothing can quench your thirst? You're desperate to find resolution. You try everything within reach. You even try substitutes, but they're just that: substitutions for the real thing—water. Sometimes we aren't just physically thirsty, but we have that deep-down, soul thirst. We're seeking something that will completely quench our parched souls. Jesus said that only He can satisfy that kind of thirst. He's here, no waiting. He can fill your life to overflowing.

Like the woman at the well, I come to You, Lord, knowing that in doing so, I will never thirst again. Amen.

Day 59

STEADFAST PRAYER

Continue in prayer, and watch in the same with thanksgiving.
COLOSSIANS 4:2 KJV

Are you the sort of person who gives up easily? Does your faith waver if God doesn't respond to your prayers right away? Don't give up, and don't stop praying, particularly if you're believing God for something that seems impossible. Be like that widow in the Bible who pestered the judge until he responded. Just keep at it. As you continue in prayer, keep a joyful heart, filled with expectation.

*I know, Lord, that You hear my prayers. Please give
me the endurance I need to keep on praying.*

Day 60

JOY IN THE JOURNEY

I press on toward the goal to win the prize for which
God has called me heavenward in Christ Jesus.
PHILIPPIANS 3:14 NIV

Ever feel like the journey's too long? Like you're not making progress? Today, ask the Lord to give you joy as you make your way toward the goal. Don't fret if things aren't happening as quickly as you want them to. Keep on pressing toward the mark. Thank Him for the process, and take time to truly take "joy in the journey."

You are the prize, Lord Jesus. Give me strength
each day to press on, I pray. Amen.

Day 61

SINGING WITH ONE ANOTHER

Speaking to one another with psalms, hymns and songs from the Spirit. Sing and make music from your heart to the Lord.
Ephesians 5:19 niv

Want to try a fun experiment? The next time someone asks you how you're doing, instead of responding, "Okay," why not get more specific? Try "I'm blessed!" or "Having an awesome day!" Encourage yourself in the Lord, and He will keep those spirits lifted. And encourage one another with words of blessing as well.

God, so many times I just trudge through life. Help me to sing Your praises and to walk each day with a spring in my step.

Day 62

STAY FOCUSED ON THE PATH

Keep your eyes focused on what is right,
and look straight ahead to what is good.
PROVERBS 4:25 NCV

Ever wonder how you can be perfectly happy one minute and upset the next? If joy is a choice, then it's one you have to make—continually. We are often ruled by our emotions, which is why it's so important to stay focused, especially when you're having a tough day. Don't let frustration steal even sixty seconds from you. Instead, choose joy!

Heavenly Father, keep my eyes fixed on You. Help me not to stray from Your presence. I ask this in Jesus' name. Amen.

Day 63

A LAMP IN THE DARKNESS

Your word is a lamp for my feet, a light on my path.
PSALM 119:105 NIV

If only life came with an instruction manual, you've said to yourself. Help for when you don't know what to do. The Bible is filled with stories of ordinary people who lived through struggles and triumphs, heartache and joy. Unlike the stories we see today on television, not every story has a happy ending. People received consequences for their erroneous actions. Through it all, God shines a light for our paths today.

Lord, help me to draw upon scripture I have memorized.
May Your Holy Word light my path.

Day 64

A JOY-FILLED TOMORROW

May he give you the desire of your heart and make all your plans succeed. May we shout for joy over your victory and lift up our banners in the name of our God.
<small>PSALM 20:4–5 NIV</small>

It's hard to have a vision for tomorrow if you're not excited about today! Each day is a gift, after all, and an opportunity to live for Christ. Today, take a stand for the things you believe in. Lift high His name. Not only will you bring joy to His heart (and your own), but you will find yourself looking forward to a joy-filled tomorrow.

Lord, I commit my plans to You. You are my Savior and my God. Help me to live for You today. Amen.

Day 65

GOD'S LOVE LETTER

The word of God is alive and active. Sharper than
any double-edged sword, it penetrates even to dividing
soul and spirit, joints and marrow; it judges
the thoughts and attitudes of the heart.

HEBREWS 4:12 NIV

The Bible is God's love letter to you. It isn't the sappy romance novel found in drugstores. The characters in those stories give only conditional love to each other. God's love is unconditional. From the first words in the book of Genesis, where God created the heavens and the earth, He is communicating His love to you. It's the love letter you've longed to read. Open it up and see for yourself.

Heavenly Father, thank You for the Bible.
I read of Your unconditional love on its pages,
and it changes my heart for the better.

Day 66

BURIED TREASURE

"The kingdom of heaven is like treasure hidden in a field.
When a man found it, he hid it again, and then in his
joy went and sold all he had and bought that field."
MATTHEW 13:44 NIV

Have you ever stumbled across a rare treasure—one so priceless that you would be willing to trade everything you own to have it? If you've given your heart to Christ, if you've accepted His work on Calvary, then you have already obtained the greatest treasure of all—new life in Him. Oh, what immeasurable joy comes from knowing He has placed that treasure in your heart for all eternity!

Lord, You are the greatest treasure one could ever
seek, and I am so glad I have found You. I am so
thankful that You live within my heart.

Day 67

REST IN JESUS

*Jesus said, "Come to me all you who are weary
and burdened, and I will give you rest."*
MATTHEW 11:28 NIV

Weary. Burdened. Need rest. Those words read like a repeating entry in a woman's daily journal. Most women feel they've earned the right to be burdened. What else but weary could they be with all they have to do? Jesus said that He would give rest to those who are weary. He would lighten our loads. Take one burden at a time and hand it over to Him. And then rest in the peace that Jesus has your life in the palm of His hands.

*Rest. Lord, it is such a beautiful word, and I find it
so rarely in these busy days. Help me to find time
to rest, I pray. My soul needs it today.*

Day 68

LIFE IS A JOURNEY

But none of these things move me, neither count I my life dear unto myself, so that I might finish my course with joy.
ACTS 20:24 KJV

The Christian life is a journey, isn't it? We move from point A to point B, and then on from there—all the while growing in our faith. Instead of focusing on the ups and downs of the journey, we should be looking ahead, to the finish line. We want to be people who finish well. Today, set your sights on that unseen line that lies ahead. What joy will come when you cross it!

Lord, I ask you to stay ever so close to me on this faith journey. I know I never walk alone. Amen.

Day 69

HEAVY BURDENS

Carry each other's burdens, and in this
way you will fulfill the law of Christ.
GALATIANS 6:2 NIV

Have you seen the size of kids' backpacks lately? Their backs sway with the weight of books, papers, and "stuff." Kids carry these packs all day on their tired shoulders. Relief comes when they drop the weighty bags at home. The burdens you carry around each day may be causing your shoulders to droop as well. Take those worries and burdens to God. He has promised to lighten your load by adding His shoulder to yours.

Lord, thank You for helping me carry the burdens of this life.
They are too much for me to bear alone. Amen.

Day 70

A STILL, SMALL VOICE

*He that hath an ear, let him hear what
the Spirit saith unto the churches.*
REVELATION 2:17 KJV

We need to "lean in" to the Lord on a daily basis. Listen to His still, small voice. Catch a glimpse of His vision for the church. Ride on the wind of the Spirit. Today, as you draw close to the Lord, listen closely. What is He speaking into your life? May your joy be full as you tune in to the voice of the Holy Spirit.

*Lord, teach me to tune out all the voices of this world
that attempt to distract me. Help me to listen
to the voice of my Good Shepherd. Amen.*

Day 71

LIVE FOR TODAY

For he shall not much remember the days of his life;
because God answereth him in the joy of his heart.
ECCLESIASTES 5:20 KJV

Sometimes we go through things that we wish we could forget. Hard things. Hurtful things. But God, in His remarkable way, eases the pain of our bumps in the road, and before long we can barely remember them. Joy rises up in place of pain, and we move forward, content in the fact that tomorrow will be better than yesterday. Don't focus on yesterday. Live for today and look forward to tomorrow.

Thank You, Lord, that Your mercies are new every
morning. You are the same yesterday, today,
and forever, and You are always with me.

Day 72

LIFE'S CHALLENGES

*Because the Sovereign LORD helps me, I will not
be disgraced. Therefore have I set my face like
flint, and I know I will not be put to shame.*
ISAIAH 50:7 NIV

Life is full of challenges. While some are short term, others last
a lifetime. What keeps you determined and motivated? Do you
seek the help of others or prefer to go it alone? Take a toddler's
approach to these challenges. As she ventures into walking,
she takes one step at a time, with help from a steady adult or
an available piece of furniture. Eventually, she walks on her
own. With God's help, take life's challenges one step at a time.

*God, together we can face any challenge life brings
my way. Thank You for helping me. Amen.*

Day 73

SEASONS OF BLESSING

There shall be showers of blessing.
Ezekiel 34:26 kjv

Don't you enjoy walking through seasons of extraordinary blessing? We can hardly believe it when God's "more than enough" provision shines down on us. What did we do to deserve it? Nothing! During such seasons, we can't forget to thank Him for the many ways He is moving in our lives. Our hearts must overflow with gratitude to a gracious and almighty God.

Lord, I will praise You all my days.
Thank You for blessing me. Amen.

Day 74

RUNNING WITH ENDURANCE

Let us run with endurance the race that is set before us,
looking unto Jesus, the author and finisher of our faith.
Hebrews 12:1–2 nkjv

Do you ever get tired of life's challenges? Do you wish you could live a carefree, predictable life? While that isn't possible, you can have a different perspective on the challenges that come your way. The Bible says we will encounter trials in this life. After all, this world is not our home; it's just a temporary residence. While we are here, though, God promises His presence, love, and comfort. He will walk beside you and give you strength to overcome whatever is in your path.

Heavenly Father, I know I am not home yet. Through the
struggles of this earthly life, I look to You for my help. Amen.

Day 75

PRAYERFUL PRAISE

Let all who seek You rejoice and be glad in You; and let those who love Your salvation say continually, "Let God be magnified!". . . You are my help and my deliverer.
PSALM 70:4–5 NKJV

Sometimes we approach God robotically: "Lord, please do this for me. Lord, please do that." We're convinced we'll be happy if only God grants our wishes, like a genie in a bottle. We're going about this backward! We should start by praising God. Thank Him for life, health, and the many answered prayers. Our joyous praise will remind us just how blessed we already are! Then—out of genuine relationship—we make our requests known.

God, I praise You for who You are. I seek our relationship before I seek Your blessing. Amen.

Day 76

JESUS' CONSTANCY

Jesus Christ is the same yesterday and today and forever.
HEBREWS 13:8 NIV

Your schedule fluctuates from day to day, and you have the calendar to prove it. Decades ago life was pretty much the same every day, especially for women. Most of what we did was for others: church and big family dinners on Sundays, wash on Mondays, ironing on Tuesdays, and so on. Aren't you glad you live in a time when you can experience new things every day? As you long for consistency, look to Jesus. His loving character never changes. He was, is, and will be.

Lord, in a world full of change, You are my one true constant. You are faithful and true. Amen.

Day 77
A FITTING REPLY

*Everyone enjoys a fitting reply; it is wonderful
to say the right thing at the right time!*
PROVERBS 15:23 NLT

Ever had a friend approach you at just the right time—say,
when you were really down—and speak something positive
and uplifting? Ah, what perfect timing! You needed to hear
something good, something pleasant. The right word at the
right time was just what the doctor ordered, causing joy to
spring up in your soul. The next time you see a friend going
through a rough time, decide to speak that "good word."

*Father, help me to be aware of others' feelings and to offer
a word of encouragement when it is needed. Amen.*

Day 78

A NEW CREATION

If anyone is in Christ, the new creation has come:
The old has gone, the new is here!
2 Corinthians 5:17 niv

The monarch butterfly begins life as a lowly caterpillar. Through the course of time, it makes itself a chrysalis and eventually turns into a beautiful butterfly. Similarly, we come to Christ with the potential to be a beautiful butterfly. Through challenges and normal life events, we go through a spiritual metamorphosis and become new creatures. We are free to fly and be what God intended us to be. His intention for you is beauty and grace. Trust Him to see you through the transformation.

Jesus, thank You for giving me new life. The old has gone. The new has come. Hallelujah!

Day 79

THERE IS MORE TO LIFE

For the kingdom of God is not meat and drink; but
righteousness, and peace, and joy in the Holy Ghost.
ROMANS 14:17 KJV

Sometimes life can be drudgery. We wake up in the morning. Get dressed. Go to work (or stay home to care for our children). We drag home in the evening, spend a little time with our loved ones, then drop into bed exhausted. Oh, there's so much more to life! The Lord wants to remind you that He has given you righteousness, peace, and joy for every day of your life! So celebrate!

Lord, no matter what I am doing, I want to honor You.
I choose to rely on You for peace and joy. Amen.

Day 80

OVERWHELMING JOY

To appoint unto them that mourn in Zion, to give unto them beauty for ashes, the oil of joy for mourning, the garment of praise for the spirit of heaviness.

ISAIAH 61:3 KJV

Seasons of mourning are difficult to bear, but praise God, He promises to give us beauty for ashes! He pours joy over us like a scented oil to woo us out of periods of grieving. Can you feel it washing down on your head even now? Can you sense the change in attitude? Slip on that garment of praise, believer! Shake off the ashes! Let God's joy overwhelm you!

Lord, bring beauty from ashes. Breathe new life into me, I pray. Amen.

Day 81

GOD GUIDES THE HUMBLE

*[The LORD] guides the humble in what
is right and teaches them his way.*
PSALM 25:9 NIV

The phrase "We're known by the company we keep" is true regardless with whom you hang around. It's also true when it's God with whom you're spending time. As you rest in His presence, read His words in the Bible, and talk to Him about all the issues of your life, you cannot help but take on some of His characteristics. He is peace, and you become more peaceful. He is good, and you take on His goodness. Your character is influenced by the company you keep.

*God, I will slow down today and spend some quality
time with You. You are truly my best friend. Amen.*

Day 82

ACTIONS REFLECT CHARACTER

We show we are servants of God by our pure lives.
2 Corinthians 6:6 ncv

Character has been defined as what one is. It's the very essence of a person. The Bible says a lot about God's character and uses phrases such as "God is love," "God is compassionate," and "God is merciful." His actions show His character. When we belong to God, we reflect His character: we are kind, loving, caring, compassionate. Our actions and behaviors reflect that character: we love, we care, we serve.

Father in heaven, may my life reflect Your character.
May others see Christ in me. Amen.

Day 83

A PRAYER OF FAITH

The prayer of faith shall save the sick,
and the Lord shall raise him up.
JAMES 5:15 KJV

Have you ever wondered why God instructed church leaders to pray for the sick? Perhaps it's because when we're sick, we often don't have the strength to pray for ourselves. We need our brothers and sisters in the Lord to cry out on our behalf. If you're struggling with illness, call for your Christian friends or church leaders to come and pray with you. What joy when healing comes!

God, I pray right now for _____ (insert the name of someone
you know who is sick). I ask that they will receive
Your healing. In Jesus' name, amen.

Day 84

GOODBYE, DISAPPOINTMENT

This hope will not lead to disappointment.
Romans 5:5 nlt

Tired of being disappointed time and time again? Ready for things to change? Try hope. Hope never leads to disappointment. When you're hopeful, you are anticipating good things, not bad. And even if the "good things" you're waiting on don't happen right away, you're energized with joy until they do. So wave goodbye to disappointment. Choose hope. Choose joy.

Lord of all, I choose hope and joy in You. Even in times of disappointment, I will look to You. Amen.

Day 85

HOPE TO
THE HOPELESS

Happy are those who are kind to the poor.
PROVERBS 14:21 NRSV

You see people in need almost every day. Whether they are hungry or hurting, the Bible says to give out of the overflow of love you have received from God. He will work through you as you serve food to those who are hungry, give clothing to those who need covering, offer hope to who feel hopeless. You can serve them with gentle words and kind deeds. Serving the powerless is a blessing in itself, but it carries a bonus—God's eternal reward.

Father, provide opportunities for me to serve, and then help me to be faithful to live out my faith. Amen.

Day 86

DINNER WITH JESUS

"Truly I tell you, whatever you did for one of the least of these brothers and sisters of mine, you did for me."
MATTHEW 25:40 NIV

What would you do if Jesus came to your house for dinner? Although you might be nervous, He would want you to be yourself, to serve Him as you would any other guest. You would give Him the best you have, out of the abundance He has provided for you. It would not matter what was served, but He would delight in your efforts on His behalf. Jesus is pleased when you serve others as you would serve Him.

Lord, may I serve others as if I were serving
You in my own home. Help me to give generously
for I have been blessed with much. Amen.

Day 87

GODLY FRIENDSHIP

"I enjoyed your friendship so much.
Your love to me was wonderful."
2 SAMUEL 1:26 NCV

Imagine finding a trunk in your attic. You've never noticed it before. It's locked, but you manage to pry it open. Inside, to your great amazement, you find gold and silver coins. Hundreds of them! That treasure is no more special—no more amazing— than finding a friend. When you find a "kindred spirit," you've discovered a priceless treasure. Oh, the joy of a godly friendship!

Thank You, Jesus, for the wonderful Christian friends
in my life. They are true treasures! Amen.

Day 88

THE GIFT OF CHILDREN

Children are a gift from God; they are his reward.
PSALM 127:3 TLB

If you're a mother, you know how precious your children are to you. They are bone of your bone, flesh of your flesh. You would not hesitate to protect them with your life. And well you should, for that's your job. Take a moment to remember that you are God's child, created in His own image. He gave His very life to save you, and even now He hovers over you protectively. Your children are God's gift to you. You are God's gift to Himself.

Lord, give me patience and a kind spirit toward children today. They are gifts from You. Amen.

Day 89

IN THE THRONE ROOM

Then will I go unto the altar of God, unto God my exceeding joy: yea, upon the harp will I praise thee, O God my God.
PSALM 43:4 KJV

We're instructed to come into the Lord's presence with a joy-filled heart to praise our way into the throne room. Perhaps you're not a musician. You don't own an instrument and only sing in the shower. Don't let that keep you from approaching the altar with a song of praise on your lips. Today, let joy lead the way, and may your praises be glorious!

Father, with all my heart, soul, and mind I praise You.
You are worthy of all praise. Amen.

Day 90

THE BEST RESOURCE

*If any of you lacks wisdom, you should ask God,
who gives generously to all without finding
fault, and it will be given to you.*

JAMES 1:5 NIV

You can read books and ask others for advice as you raise your children, but how can you be assured that what you're doing is the best for them? Just as your children come to you with questions, take your questions to God, your heavenly Father. No question is too small or too big. You can't stump Him, because He knows you and your children intimately. After all, He has created all of you. God is the best resource you can find.

*Giver of wisdom, provide it for me, I pray.
I want to be wise in Your ways. Amen.*

Day 91

JOY IN THE EVERYDAY

"For in him we live and move and have our being."
ACTS 17:28 NIV

Every breath we breathe comes from God. Every step we take is a gift from our Creator. We can do nothing apart from Him. In the same sense, God goes through every joy and every sorrow with us. His heart is for us. We can experience joy in our everyday lives, even when things aren't going our way. We simply have to remember that He is in control. We have our being in Him!

Creator God, You breathed life into the first man and the first woman. Help me to realize You are in control. You gave me my very life! Amen.

Day 92

CHOOSE GOD, CHOOSE LIFE

"Choose life and not death!"
2 KINGS 18:32 NIV

No matter how good—or bad—your choices have been in your life, there is really just one choice that matters. That is the choice of where you will spend eternity. God has given you a free will, and He expects you to use it. You must choose Him—consciously, intentionally choose Him—or you will be making a choice by default, a choice against Him. The Bible says it's a life and death matter. Your free will is His gift to you—use it!

Father in heaven, I have chosen to follow Jesus, and I will choose Him again every day of my life. Amen.

Day 93

OIL OF JOY

Let thy garments be always white;
and let thy head lack no ointment.
ECCLESIASTES 9:8 KJV

What do the words "oil of joy" (Isaiah 61:3 KJV) mean to you? Can you envision the Lord anointing you with that precious oil? Do you feel it running over your head and down your cheeks? Oh, that we would always sense the joy of His anointing. That we would see ourselves as usable in the kingdom. Today, as you enter your prayer time, allow the Lord to saturate you with His oil of joy.

Lord, anoint me for Your service.
Use me to expand Your kingdom. Amen.

Day 94

ECHOING PRAISE

Make a joyful noise unto the LORD, all ye lands.
PSALM 100:1 KJV

How do we praise God for His many blessings? If we follow the pattern of Old Testament saints, then we lift our voices in thanksgiving! We let others know. With a resounding voice, we echo our praises, giving thanks for all He has done and all He continues to do. So praise Him today! Make a joyful noise!

Lord, I thank You for all that You are and
all that You have done. I praise Your name
for that which You will continue to do. Amen.

Day 95

BE A GOD PLEASER

To the person who pleases him, God gives wisdom, knowledge and happiness, but to the sinner he gives the task of gathering and storing up wealth to hand it over to the one who pleases God. This too is meaningless, a chasing after the wind.
ECCLESIASTES 2:26 NIV

Have you ever watched someone chase after fame, fortune, or wealth? Maybe you've secretly longed for those same things. Instead of chasing after the things this world can offer, which are nothing more than wind, chase after God. Be a God pleaser. Store up His treasures. He is the giver of all things and will make sure you have all you need—and more. What joy in finding that treasure!

God, I chase after You. The things of this world will not last. I find my joy in You. Amen.

Day 96
CHOOSING GOD

"Choose this day whom you will serve. . .but as for me and my household, we will serve the Lord."
JOSHUA 24:15 NRSV

From the mundane to the life-altering, we make choices every day. Do you wish you could see into the future and know which direction your life will take if you make this or that choice? Perhaps it's for the best that we don't have that option. But you can put your trust in the One who does. Listen to the Lord; choose Him. When you do, it will be much easier to make the right choices for your life.

Like Joshua, I commit to serve You, God. As for me and my family, we will serve You, Lord. Amen.

Day 97

GOD AS COMFORTER

The LORD will hear your crying, and he will comfort you.
When he hears you, he will help you.
ISAIAH 30:19 NCV

The Christian life is difficult—and emotional. It was for Jesus' disciples also. Jesus knew His death would be the most emotional moment of their lives. So just before Jesus gave His life on the cross, He sat down with them, explained that He would be leaving, and promised that He would send another Comforter, the Holy Spirit. He has placed His Comforter inside of you. He hears every cry.

Lord, one day there will be no more tears. I am thankful
that, for now, while I suffer on this earth, You have
sent Your Spirit to comfort me. Amen.

Day 98

THE PERFECT RECIPE FOR HAPPINESS

*You have greatly encouraged me and made
me happy despite all our troubles.*
2 CORINTHIANS 7:4 NLT

Want to know the perfect recipe for happiness? Spend your days focused on making others happy. If you shift your focus from yourself to others, you accomplish two things: You put others first, and you're always looking for ways to make others smile. There's something about spreading joy that satisfies the soul.

*God, make me an encourager. Help me to
shift my focus from self to others. Amen.*

Day 99

THE GIFT OF SCRIPTURE

*Whatsoever things were written aforetime were written
for our learning, that we through patience and
comfort of the scriptures might have hope.*
ROMANS 15:4 KJV

God has given you another invaluable gift filled with His love
and comfort—the Holy Scriptures. As you read about Noah,
Abraham, Jacob, Joseph, Moses, Esther, Ruth, Job, David, Eli-
jah, Mary, and Paul, you will see how God comforted them in
their darkest hours. He will certainly do the same for you. Be
encouraged as you read, and place your hope in His goodness.
He will comfort you, and you can be sure of that.

*Lord, just as you comforted those who came before me,
I pray for Your goodness in my life. Amen.*

Day 100

BURIED ALIVE

The LORD is my strength and my shield;
my heart trusts in him, and he helps me.
My heart leaps for joy and with my song I praise him.
PSALM 28:7 NIV

Sometimes our sorrows run deep. We can feel buried alive. That's why it's so important to allow our joys to run deep too. Today, as you ponder the many things you have to be thankful for, pause a moment. Take a comforting breath. Thank God— from the bottom of your heart—for the deep joys in your life.

Lord, I pause now to thank You for the joy You have placed in my life through _____ (finish this prayer by speaking many of the blessings that have come from God's hand).

Day 101

COMMITMENT ISSUES

"May your hearts be fully committed to the LORD our God, to live by his decrees and obey his commands, as at this time."
1 KINGS 8:61 NIV

Many women have issues with commitment. Their fear of failure causes them to drift in and out of relationships, jobs, and obligations without ever really settling anywhere. Committing your life first to God will help you commit later to others. Give Him your love, your life, your heart, and ask Him to help you walk out your commitment one day at a time. Everything else will follow.

Help me, Lord, to be faithful and committed to You. You are so faithful to me. Amen.

Day 102

A HOPEFUL FUTURE

*Now faith is confidence in what we hope for
and assurance about what we do not see.*
HEBREWS 11:1 NIV

You must look at your future as hopeful and filled with wonderful "what ifs." No, you're not promised tomorrow. But if you give up on your hopes and dreams, if you lose sight of the plans the Lord has laid on your heart, they will surely not come to pass. Trust God to make the invisible visible. And in the meantime, rejoice! You have a lot to look forward to!

*God, I am so thankful for the hope I have in You.
I know all Your plans are good. Amen.*

Day 103

THE PAIN OF CHILDBIRTH

"A woman giving birth to a child has pain because her time has come; but when her baby is born she forgets the anguish because of her joy that a child is born into the world."
JOHN 16:21 NIV

If you've ever delivered a child, you know the pain associated with childbirth. But that's not what you remember after the fact, is it? No, as you hold that little one in your arms, only one thing remains—the supernatural joy you experience as you gaze into your newborn's eyes. The same is true with the seasons we walk through. Sorrows will end, and joy will rise to the surface once again!

God, may I remember that Your mercies are new every morning. Sorrow is for a time, but joy comes in the morning!

Day 104

BALANCING COMMITMENTS

Commit everything you do to the Lord.
PSALM 37:5 TLB

Some women can't commit, while others overcommit. Even when your intentions are good, you can bring down your whole house of cards by trying to juggle too many things—family, social events, work, spiritual time. Soon you find yourself with no personal time, becoming more stressed by the moment. Ask God to help you balance your commitments in a way that is healthy for you. Then you will be free to meet your commitments head-on and accomplish them with excellence.

Lord, help me to say no when I need to, and help me to be committed to the things I say yes to. Amen.

Day 105

BOOMERANG

"When I smiled at them, they could hardly believe it;
their faces lit up, their troubles took wing!"
JOB 29:24 MSG

Some folks are natural joy givers. They thrive on bringing joy
to others in their world. If that's your nature, then you need to
know that God wants you to receive joy too. It's a dual process.
When you give it, like a boomerang, it comes back to you! So
toss out some joy today. It will surely return, filling your heart
and bringing a smile to your face!

Lord, I am so thankful that I have joy because of You.
Happiness is fleeting, but joy is found in Your presence! Amen.

Day 106

GIVE WHAT YOU HAVE RECEIVED

You, Lord, are a compassionate and gracious God,
slow to anger, abounding in love and faithfulness.
PSALM 86:15 NIV

God never asks you to do anything for someone else that He has not already done for you. You are able to show compassion for others because He has shown compassion for you. When you were lost and lonely, He found you. When you were sick with sin, He forgave you. When your life was in shambles, He held you close and comforted you. When you longed for a fresh start, He opened the way before you. You give from what you have already received.

Lord, give me a heart of compassion for those
in need. You have been so merciful to me.

Day 107

THE PATH OF LIFE

*"You have made known to me the paths of life;
you will fill me with joy in your presence."*
ACTS 2:28 NIV

God gives us everything we need to make it through life. He teaches us His ways. Fills us with His joy. Gives us the pleasure of meeting with Him for times of intimate worship. What an awesome Teacher and Friend. He takes us by the hand and gently leads us—from experience to experience, joy to joy.

*Thank You, Jesus, for taking me by the hand and leading
me through life. I find such joy in Your presence. Amen.*

Day 108

SATURATED WITH HOPE

May the God of hope fill you with all joy and peace
as you trust in him, so that you may overflow
with hope by the power of the Holy Spirit.
ROMANS 15:13 NIV

Isn't it fun to think about God pouring joy into our lives? Imagine yourself with a water pitcher in hand, pouring out, out, out—covering everything in sight. The Lord wants us, through the power of the Spirit, to overflow. To bubble over. To experience not just joy, but hope—a benefit of joy. Today, as you spend time in prayer, allow God to saturate you with His joyous hope.

God, You don't offer me a tiny portion of joy, hope, and peace.
You give to me abundantly, over and above any expectation.
Thank You, Lord. Amen.

Day 109

ALWAYS HELP

*Never walk away from someone who deserves help;
your hand is God's hand for that person.*
PROVERBS 3:28 MSG

The Bible reminds us that we are God's hands and feet. We carry His compassion to the world around us. What a wonderful privilege and responsibility. Ask God to open your eyes to the people around you who need His merciful touch, His gentle encouragement, His tender intervention. You won't be able to meet all the needs you see, but if you're asking, He will show you where you can make a difference. And when you raise another's head, you raise your own as well.

*I want to be the hands and feet of Jesus to those around
me. Show me today, Lord, the people I need to help.*

Day 110

A PRICELESS JEWEL

*Joyful is the person who finds wisdom,
the one who gains understanding.*
PROVERBS 3:13 NLT

Imagine you've lost a priceless jewel—one passed down from your grandmother to your mother and then to you. You search everywhere, under every rock, in every closet. Still, you can't find it. Finally, in the least likely spot, you discover it! Joy floods your soul! Now imagine that "jewel" is wisdom. You've stumbled across it, and oh, what a treasure! Talk about a happy find!

*God, please give me wisdom that I might
understand You in a greater way. Amen.*

Day 111

GOD'S PROVISION

"Who provides food for the raven when its young cry
out to God and wander about for lack of food?"
JOB 38:41 NIV

Does it fill your heart with joy to know that God provides for your needs? He makes provision—in both seasons of want and seasons of plenty. There's no need to strive. No need to worry. He has everything under control. If He provides food for the ravens, then surely He knows how to give you everything you need when you need it. So praise Him!

God, thank You for always meeting my needs. I trust and rest
in Your provision for me both physically and spiritually. Amen.

Day 112

YOU ARE ENOUGH

In quietness and in confidence shall be your strength.
ISAIAH 30:15 KJV

Confidence is really just the quiet assurance that you are enough—enough of an employee to get the job done, enough of a wife and mother to take care of your family, enough of a woman of God to accomplish what He has called you to do. For some women, that comes easily; for others, not so much. If your confidence is lagging, reach out to God for help. He will help you unveil the real you—the confident and assured you.

You are my confidence, Lord.
Fill me with Your strength. Amen.

Day 113

BE FOUND FAITHFUL

A faithful man shall abound with blessings.
PROVERBS 28:20 KJV

To *abound* means to have more than enough. When you're abounding, all of your needs are met—and then some! How wonderful to go through such seasons. So what do we have to do to qualify for these "more than enough" blessings? Only one thing. Be found faithful. Trust God during the lean seasons. Don't give up! Then, when the "abounding" seasons come, you can truly rejoice!

May I be found as faithful, Lord, in lean
seasons as when blessings abound. Amen.

Day 114

CONFIDENT, NOT PERFECT

Such confidence we have through Christ before God.
Not that we are competent in ourselves to claim anything
for ourselves, but our competence comes from God.
2 CORINTHIANS 3:4–5 NIV

As a child of God, you should be confident about who you are—not pushy or overbearing—a woman who knows she is the daughter of the great and mighty King. Draw your confidence from your relationship with your heavenly Father, and then take life one challenge at a time. Life isn't about being perfect. It's about being sure of whom you believe in and who you are in Him.

Lord, through You I stand in confidence. I call out
Your name when I am weak, and You come quickly
to me and give me strength. Amen.

Day 115

A GRATEFUL HEART

*Give, and it shall be given unto you; good measure,
pressed down, and shaken together, and running over,
shall men give into your bosom.*

LUKE 6:38 KJV

"Give, and it shall be given unto you." Likely, if you've been walking with the Lord for any length of time, you've heard this dozens of times. Do we give so that we can get? No, we give out of a grateful heart, and the Lord—in His generosity—meets our needs. Today, pause and thank Him for the many gifts He has given you. Do you feel the joy running over?

*Out of the abundant blessings You have
given to me, I give in return. Amen.*

Day 116

EMBRACING LIFE

I say it is better to be content with what little you have.
Otherwise, you will always be struggling for more,
and that is like chasing the wind.

ECCLESIASTES 4:6 NCV

When it comes to evaluating your life, God's scales weigh differently than yours. Seen through His eyes, the smallest things can bring you the deepest joy. When you embrace your life just as it is, you can lay down the struggle for what might be or might have been. You can feel the blessing of contentment that, for this moment, your life is the perfect starting place for the next step in the journey.

Give me contentment, Lord, so that I might not chase after more, more, more. What a waste of time that is! Amen.

Day 117

EXCESS OF BLESSING

*And my God will meet all your needs according
to the riches of his glory in Christ Jesus.*
PHILIPPIANS 4:19 NIV

Sometimes God goes overboard when it's time to make provision.
He blesses us above and beyond what we could ask or think.
He not only meets our needs, but He throws in a bit of excess
just to see us smile. If you're in a season of abundant provision,
remember to share the joy! Pass on a portion of what He has
given you. And praise Him! What an awesome God we serve!

*Lord, just as the disciples gathered twelve baskets of
leftovers after You fed five thousand, You go above
and beyond in my life. Thank You for Your blessings!*

Day 118

SIMPLE THANKFULNESS

I have learned to be content with whatever I have.
PHILIPPIANS 4:11 NRSV

Having what you want or wanting what you have—it's amazing what a difference the order of those simple words can make. What a gift it is to feel that sense of having enough, not to always be wanting more, to believe that God has given what you truly need. As you focus today on the pockets of your life that you "wouldn't have any other way," whisper a prayer of thanks. Take a breath and let this moment be full, just on its own.

Father in heaven, I rest my head on my pillow in peace. I am content where I am and with what You have given to me. Amen.

Day 119

TRY WISDOM

He who heeds the word wisely will find good,
and whoever trusts in the LORD, happy is he.
PROVERBS 16:20 NKJV

Want the key to true happiness? Try wisdom. When others around you are losing their heads, losing their cool, and losing sleep over their decisions, choose to react differently. Step up to the plate. Handle matters wisely. Wise choices always lead to joyous outcomes. And along the way, you will be setting an example for others around you to follow. So c'mon, get happy! Get wisdom!

Help me, Lord, to make wise choices that will honor You. Amen.

Day 120

HELPING THE LESS FORTUNATE

"I will abundantly bless her provision;
I will satisfy her needy with bread."
PSALM 132:15 NASB

The Lord has promised to meet all of our needs according to His riches in glory. His heart is for His people, especially the poor and downtrodden. Today, as you seek God about your own needs, ask Him how you can help meet the needs of the less fortunate in your community. What a joy it will be to reach out to others—even if you're also in need.

God, help me to see and meet the needs of those
around me. There is great blessing in giving.

Day 121

YOU DON'T FACE
IT ALONE

*LORD, you are my shield, my wonderful
God who gives me courage.*
PSALM 3:3 NCV

You never know where courage will pop up in your life, because you never know what you'll face that will require it. You can be sure, though, that God will give you courage when you need it. God is both your protector and your strength. So be confident that whatever you face, you do not face it alone. You face today with resources both from your own soul and the Spirit who dwells within you.

*God, when I go into battle, I do so with courage
because You are always on my side.*

Day 122

A CITIZEN OF HEAVEN

"In the world you have tribulation, but take courage; I have overcome the world."
JOHN 16:33 NASB

While living in this world that you can touch and see, you must remember you are also part of a world that can be known only through faith. In the physical world around you, you face disappointment and struggle, yes. But as a citizen of the kingdom of heaven, you are blessed with a greater power—Someone who advocates for you. Jesus never claimed you would be without struggle, but He always reminds His followers of the victory that is waiting.

Lord, help me to remember that this is not my true home. One day I will be with You in heaven.

Day 123

PREPARE FOR VICTORY

Then they returned, every man of Judah and
Jerusalem, and Jehoshaphat in the forefront of them,
to go again to Jerusalem with joy; for the LORD had
made them to rejoice over their enemies.
2 CHRONICLES 20:27 KJV

Enemy forces were just around the bend. Jehoshaphat, king of Judah, called his people together. After much prayer, he sent the worshippers (the Levites) to the front lines, singing joyful praises as they went. The battle was won! When you face your next battle, praise your way through it! Strength and joy will rise up within you! Prepare for victory!

God, You are victorious over all.
Thank You for fighting my battles! Amen.

Day 124

PERFECT UNITY

Then make my joy complete by being like-minded, having the same love, being one in spirit and of one mind.
PHILIPPIANS 2:2 NIV

Want to know how to bring joy to God's heart? Live in unity with your Christian brothers and sisters. When we're like-minded, our heavenly Father is pleased. Are there problems to be ironed out with a Christian friend? Troubles in your church family? Let this be the day you fulfill His joy by resolving those differences. Let unity lead the way!

God, help me to seek reconciliation with those I am at odds with today. I want to live in unity with other believers. Amen.

Day 125

STRENGTHENING YOUR ROOTS

Just as you received Christ Jesus as Lord, continue to live your lives in him, rooted and built up in him, strengthened in the faith as you were taught, and overflowing with thankfulness.

COLOSSIANS 2:6–7 NIV

Even though you don't always see progress in your walk with God, you can be sure that your roots are going down deep. Beneath the soil, God tends your faith—the longer you walk with Him, the deeper His hold on you. You came to Him with nothing and simply surrendered to His love. And that is all it takes—just a willingness to keep walking with Him and trusting that He is strengthening your roots beneath you.

Jesus, I want to live my life for you and be strong in my faith. I want my life to be rooted in You for all my days. Amen.

Day 126

HOPE AND JOY

For what is our hope, or joy, or crown of rejoicing? Is it not even you in the presence of our Lord Jesus Christ at His coming?
1 Thessalonians 2:19 nkjv

Isn't it interesting how the words *hope* and *joy* seem to fit together? You rarely find one without the other. If you have hope in the unseen tomorrow, then joy rises up in your soul to give you strength for the journey. Spend time in God's holy presence today. In that place, you will find both hope and joy.

Lord, I pause now to spend time in Your Word and in Your holy presence. Fill me with Your hope, joy, and peace.

Day 127

WORSHIP AND WONDER

Praise ye the Lord. Praise God in his sanctuary:
praise him in the firmament of his power.
PSALM 150:1 KJV

There's something amazing about being in a powerful worship service when all of God's children are like-minded, lifting up their voices in joyful chorus. The next time you're in such a service, pause a moment and listen—really listen. Can you sense the joy that sweeps across the room? The wonder? Oh, what a powerful force we are when we praise in one accord!

I will praise You all the days of my life, Lord. I love to praise
You with other believers and when I am all alone.

Day 128

STAYING ON THE PATH

Be very careful, then, how you live—not as unwise but as wise.
Ephesians 5:15 niv

As you walk with the Lord each day, you will face many crossroads. God will open the way before you, but He will not mandate your steps. He has given you a free will with which to choose the steps you take. He does admonish you to choose wisely though. The safest way to do that is to keep your hand in God's hand at all times. He will never let you wander off the path. Reach out to Him and He'll be there.

There are so many paths to choose from, Father,
but I want to stay on the right one. Guide me, I pray.

Day 129

SYMBOLIC CRUCIFIXION

I am crucified with Christ: nevertheless I live;
yet not I, but Christ liveth in me.
GALATIANS 2:20 KJV

When you gave your heart to Christ, the old you—the person you used to be—died. She's no longer alive. In a symbolic sense, you rose up out of that experience with God as a new creature—never again the same. So the life you now live isn't really your own. It's His! And He lives in you. What a joyful exchange!

May I shine for You each day of my life, Lord,
as I submit wholly to You. Amen.

Day 130

HAVING A PLAN

The human mind plans the way, but the LORD directs the steps.
PROVERBS 16:9 NRSV

It's always good to have a plan. It's also good to acknowledge that plans change—and sometimes those detours actually lead us to a better way. Make your lists, set your priorities, perfect your agendas, and work them well. But in the midst of it all, remember to surrender them to God. Then sit back and watch what your willing and prepared heart can do in the light of His direction.

God, may I hold on to my plans loosely.
I want to live out Your will for my life.

Day 131

MAKING PROVISIONS

*"He provides you with plenty of food
and fills your hearts with joy."*
ACTS 14:17 NIV

When we think about provision, we usually think in terms of money, don't we? Getting the bills paid. Having food in the pantry. Making sure our needs are met. But what about our emotional needs? Does the Lord make provision in that area as well? Of course! According to Acts 14:17, He fills our hearts with joy. What an awesome God we serve!

*Thank You for Your daily provision for my needs, Lord.
May I learn to trust You day by day. Amen.*

Day 132

SPIRITUAL REGENERATION

"Who has known the mind of the Lord so as to instruct him?" But we have the mind of Christ.
1 CORINTHIANS 2:16 NIV

When you receive Christ, you are regenerated spiritually and given a renewed way of thinking. The Spirit of God makes His home in you. You have the mind of Christ. Given all that, shouldn't this life be easy? Shouldn't you always know what to do? Not necessarily. You still have your own nature and will, but you also have a resource to turn to. As you quiet yourself and learn to hear the mind of Christ within you, the way does become clearer.

Lord Jesus, may I see the world the way You desire me to see it. I want to have the mind of Christ. Amen.

Day 133

GIVING THANKS

Let us continually offer the sacrifice of praise to God, that is,
the fruit of our lips, giving thanks to His name.
HEBREWS 13:15 NKJV

What do you think of when you hear the word *giving*? Money?
Gifts? Offerings? Time? Talents? Treasures? One of the things
we're called to give is thanks! That's right. So pause a moment
and thank God for His many blessings in your life. Feels good
to give, doesn't it?

Show me today, heavenly Father, how
I might give out of my many blessings.

Day 134

BEING FULLY SATISFIED

The desires of the diligent are fully satisfied.
PROVERBS 13:4 NIV

It's a fact of life that you don't always get what you want. You've been learning that lesson since you were two and the floor wasn't too far away to stage a tantrum. But now that you are pretty far from the floor, you have to remember that there's a difference between having everything you want and being satisfied. God doesn't promise to fulfill your every craving, but if you live life in relationship to Him, you will be satisfied—fully satisfied.

Father, every good and perfect gift comes from You. May I realize how blessed I am and be satisfied with Your provision for me. Thank You! Amen.

Day 135

TRUE JOY

"Blessed are the merciful, for they shall obtain mercy."
MATTHEW 5:7 NKJV

In some ways, mercy is like forgiveness. God offers it to the same extent we're willing to give it to others. The more merciful we are to those who wrong us, the more merciful God is to us. And blessings flow out of relationships that extend mercy. Want to experience true joy today? Give—and receive—mercy.

Father, my soul craves true joy. Help me to be generous in mercy so I may receive Your heavenly blessing. Amen.

Day 136

YOUR HEART'S DESIRE

Delight yourself in the LORD, and he will
give you the desires of your heart.
PSALM 37:4 ESV

What does your heart desire? How much of your mental space does that desire occupy? The teachings of the Bible address the irony of the desires of our hearts. When we focus our attention on God, good things come to us. Even those things we want the most. It's easy to think you should do the opposite—fight for what you want. The twist in the plot is that when you delight in God, your heart's desires are most easily met.

May I desire You above all else, Lord; and may I take
great joy in You. You will take care of the rest. Amen.

Day 137

HEAVENLY CELEBRATION

"In the same way, there is more joy in heaven over one lost sinner who repents and returns to God than over ninety-nine others who are righteous and haven't strayed away!"
LUKE 15:7 NLT

What a party heaven throws when one person comes to know the Lord! Can't you see it now? The angels let out a shout. The trumpeters play their victory chant. All of heaven reacts joyfully to the news. Oh, that we would respond with such joy to the news of a lost soul turning to the Lord. What a celebration!

Jesus, reveal to me those who need to know You. Then give me boldness to share Your saving work in my life. Amen.

Day 138

USING YOUR TALENTS

*"You must present as the Lord's portion the best
and holiest part of everything given to you."*
NUMBERS 18:29 NIV

Christians are called to give of their time, talents, and treasures.
Think about the time God has given you. What time can you
give back, and how? And what about your talents? Ask the
Lord to show you how to use them to advance the kingdom.
And your treasures? If you're struggling with giving to your
local church, make this the day you release your hold on your
finances. Give the Lord your very best.

*Lord, help me to remember to give to You of my firstfruits—
not my leftovers. In Jesus' name I pray. Amen.*

Day 139

REPLACING YOUR SORROWS

Yet I will rejoice in the LORD, I will joy in the God of my salvation.
HABAKKUK 3:18 NKJV

Perhaps you've been waiting on pins and needles for something to happen—a promised promotion, an amazing opportunity, something wonderful. Instead, you get bad news. Things aren't going to pan out the way you expected. What do you do now? Instead of giving in to disappointment, continue to rejoice in the Lord and watch the disappointment lift. He will replace your sorrows with great joy.

I will trust in You, Father, and in Your will and timeline for my life. I will find my joy in You alone. Amen.

Day 140

LOSING YOUR RESOLVE

"As for you, be strong and do not give up,
for your work will be rewarded."
2 CHRONICLES 15:7 NIV

What is it that's threatening to make you lose your resolve and give up? Maybe it's exhaustion or discouragement. It might be niggling questions like "Is this worth it? Is anyone going to notice?" The Bible promises over and over again that your determination will be rewarded. God sees even if no one else does. He understands the process and the difficulty. He will be waiting at the finish line, and your efforts in this life will be well worth it.

Strengthen me, Lord, that I might endure
and finish the race set before me.

Day 141

MAKING PROMISES

Let us hold fast the confession of our hope without
wavering, for He who promised is faithful.
HEBREWS 10:23 NKJV

Faithfulness is in short supply these days. People make promises, but circumstances change. Life twists and turns. But God is faithful. The promises He has made, He will keep. You don't always know how and when, and sometimes life can mislead you into thinking your hope is lost. But if you are determined to hold on, the fog will eventually clear and your course will become clear. God is counting on you to stay the course and never give up.

You are a promise keeper, God. Many people will
disappoint me, but in You I find a steadfast
Lord who never changes or lets me down.

Day 142

CONTAGIOUS GOOD NEWS

*How lovely on the mountains are the feet of him
who brings good news, who announces peace
and brings good news of happiness.*

ISAIAH 52:7 NASB

Ever had a contagious sickness? Something like chicken pox or measles? Maybe a bad cold? Surely you did your best not to share it with your friends and coworkers. Joy is a lot like that. It's contagious. You can spread it without even meaning to. Pretty soon all of your Christian brothers and sisters are catching it. Now, that's one virus you don't need to worry about—so spread the joy!

*I want to overflow with the Good News in such a way
that it is "caught" by those around me. Make me
a faithful witness of Your salvation, Jesus.*

Day 143

LOSING SELF-FOCUS

*"Love the LORD your God with all your heart and
with all your soul and with all your strength."*
DEUTERONOMY 6:5 NIV

We talk about loving someone from the heart, but loving someone actually takes all of us. We don't just love God with our hearts. We love Him with our hearts, our souls, and our strength—we love Him with our whole selves. That's the kind of love He wants from you. You can lose your own self-focus in giving that kind of whole-self devotion, and losing your self-focus is what a surrendered life is all about.

Help me to remove my focus from self, Lord. Remind me to turn my eyes upon You and look full in Your wonderful face.

Day 144

NO GREATER JOY

Then my soul will rejoice in the LORD and delight in his salvation.
PSALM 35:9 NIV

Do you remember what it felt like to put your trust in Christ for the first time? Likely, you've never experienced anything else that brought such joy, such release. Oh, the joy of that salvation experience. The overwhelming realization that the God of the universe loves you—enough to send His only Son to die on a cross so that you could have eternal life. There's no greater joy than the joy of salvation.

Renew my heart today, Lord Jesus, with the joy of salvation. You have saved me from sin! Hallelujah!

Day 145

ROOM IN YOUR HEART

Guard my life, for I am faithful to you; save your servant who trusts in you. You are my God.
PSALM 86:2 NIV

Devotion to God comes with strings attached—or maybe it would be better to say promises. When you give yourself completely to God, you become an heir to eternal life and a child of His kingdom. Success is guaranteed in whatever you do because you are carrying out His will. Give Him every room in your heart. Open every door wide and invite Him in. When He comes, He brings with Him peace, joy, love, and much more.

Lord, I invite You to take up residence in every nook and cranny of my heart. You are my God.

Day 146

SEEK OUT WISDOM

*I applied mine heart to know, and to
search, and to seek out wisdom.*
ECCLESIASTES 7:25 KJV

Remember when you participated in your first Easter egg hunt?
You searched under every bush, every tree until you found one
of those colorful eggs. The quest for wisdom is much like that.
You have to look under a lot of shrubs to find it, especially in this
day and age. Oh, but what a prize! Today, as you apply your heart
to the Word of God, seek out wisdom. What a joyous treasure!

*I seek You, Lord, in the morning, at noon, and before I
go to sleep at night. I seek You with all my heart.*

Day 147

FEELING UNHEARD

You, Lord, hear the desire of the afflicted; you encourage them, and you listen to their cry.
PSALM 10:17 NIV

It's easy to feel unheard in this life. Even those closest to you may sometimes fail to listen. But God hears. He's never too tired, too busy, too distracted. You don't need an appointment. He's always listening, always encouraging. So cry out to Him. Share everything with Him—those things that cause you pain, those things that bring you joy. Let Him in on your secrets and your hopes. He will never fail you.

Thank You, Lord, that You not only hear me, but You really listen. You know the desires of my heart, and You know every trouble.

Day 148

ENDURING MERCY

O give thanks unto the LORD; for he is good:
for his mercy endureth for ever.
PSALM 136:1 KJV

God's mercy endures forever. It never ends. What about our mercy? How long does it endure? Until our patience is tested? Until someone rubs us the wrong way? Until we're hurt or offended by a friend or coworker? If God's mercy endures forever, we should strive to be merciful too. After all, if the King of kings offers it repetitively, shouldn't we do so as well? Today, extend mercy and watch the joy flow!

Merciful Lord, fill me with mercy for others—
a mercy so generous that it can come only from You.
In Jesus' name, amen.

Day 149

REJOICE IN THE LORD ALWAYS

Rejoice in the Lord always.
Again I will say, rejoice!
PHILIPPIANS 4:4 NKJV

Have you ever had to repeat yourself to a child, a spouse, or a coworker? When we want to get our point across—or think someone's not listening as he or she should—we repeat our words. God knows what it's like! Some things are worth repeating just because they're so good. "Rejoice in the Lord always. . .and again I say, rejoice!" Paul tells us not just once, but twice. Better listen up!

Lord, I will rejoice in You again and again.
All my days I will find my joy in You.

Day 150

ENCOURAGING YOUR COMMUNITY

*Think of ways to motivate one another
to acts of love and good works.*
HEBREWS 10:24 NLT

The great thing about Christian community is that we inspire each other in this Christian walk. Haven't you caught someone red-handed in some kind of faithful act and felt inspired? And who knows how many times your faith has been spotted and someone made a better choice "next time" because they saw the choice you made. That's the wonder of rubbing elbows in the fray together. Faith alone strengthens you. But faith together inspires more faith!

*Thank You, Lord, for Christian friends. I do not run this race
alone. Strengthen my faith community, I pray. Amen.*

Day 151

GUARD YOUR TONGUE

She speaks with wisdom, and faithful
instruction is on her tongue.
PROVERBS 31:26 NIV

Have you ever known someone who epitomized wisdom?
What set her apart from others of your acquaintance? A truly
wise person thinks carefully before speaking and only opens
her mouth when wisdom is ready to flow out. Kindness is on
her tongue. There's great joy in "becoming" wise in this way.
Today, guard your tongue. Think before you speak. By doing
so, you bring joy to others—and to yourself.

Give me wisdom, Lord. Help me to guard
my tongue and think before I speak.

Day 152

LIFE IS FLEETING

God so loved the world that he gave his one and only Son, that whoever believes in him shall not perish but have eternal life.
JOHN 3:16 NIV

Life here on earth is fleeting. One day we are sitting on the floor playing with our favorite dolls, and then we find ourselves grown-up women, dealing with grown-up issues. In what seems like a moment, we notice wrinkles around our eyes and gray hair tickling the borders of our youthful faces. Life happens, and that's why God created a way for us to live on, free from time and age. Through His Son, He bought eternal life for you. What greater gift could there be?

I am thankful for eternal life, Lord. Death has lost its sting because I am a believer in Christ.

Day 153

DO A HEART CHECK

A happy heart makes the face cheerful,
but heartache crushes the spirit.
PROVERBS 15:13 NIV

Have you ever been so disappointed, so broken down, that you felt you couldn't go on? Don't despair! Even in the hardest of times, it's possible to have a glad heart. The body reacts to the spirit, so if you want to keep on keepin' on, better do a heart check! No doubt, the cheerful expression on your face is sure to make others ask, "What's her secret?"

Please give me an eternally happy heart, Lord. Through
all of life's circumstances, may I find my joy in You.

Day 154

OCCUPYING THE HEAVENLY KINGDOM

"My sheep listen to my voice; I know them, and they follow me. I give them eternal life, and they will never die, and no one can steal them out of my hand."

John 10:27–28 NCV

In eternity we will have no need of protection. All will be well as we occupy the heavenly kingdom. But here on earth, there are many hazards. God has not left your eternal life to chance. He purchased it for you with the sacrifice of His own Son. Then, He Himself watches over you so that nothing and no one can keep you from reaching your destination. The life God has given you is not up for the taking. It is sealed by His promise.

Good Shepherd, thank You that I have eternal security and protection in You. May I always heed the sound of Your voice. Amen.

Day 155

KINDNESS BRINGS HAPPINESS

*It is a sin to hate your neighbor, but being
kind to the needy brings happiness.*
Proverbs 14:21 NCV

Our loving heavenly Father is so merciful toward us, and He expects us to treat others with mercy too. Did you realize that having mercy on those who are less fortunate than you can actually make you happy? It's true! Reach out to someone today—and watch the joy start to flow!

*Lord, it is a beautiful blessing to give to those in need.
Show me ways I can give to others so I can watch
the joy flow from one person to the next.*

Day 156

SETTING AN EXAMPLE

Be an example to the believers with your words,
your actions, your love, your faith, and your pure life.
1 Timothy 4:12 ncv

Setting an example for others can seem like a heavy weight—always having to watch your words and your actions. Being good on your own is a simple impossibility. There's only one way that you can live worthy to represent God. That is by letting Him live through you. When your self-interest crowds to the forefront, surrender yourself to Him. Soon you will find yourself demonstrating for others that it's possible to live a pure and godly life.

Father, I want to be a shining example for You in this dark
world. May I be salt and light. May others see You in me. Amen.

Day 157

GIFTS AT CHURCH

*Just as a body, though one, has many parts, but all
its many parts form one body, so it is with Christ.*
1 Corinthians 12:12 niv

It's fun to look around the church on any given Sunday morning and see the various gifts at work. One teaches, the other leads worship. One edifies, another handles the finances. God didn't make us all alike. Praise Him for that! He recognizes our differences. How do we merge all of those unique people into one body? We don't! That's God's job. We simply do our best to remain unified members of a joyous family.

*Lord, it is such a blessing to know that Your church is many
parts but one body. How I love the body of Christ!*

Day 158

SEEING JESUS IN YOU

*Provide people with a glimpse of good
living and of the living God.*
PHILIPPIANS 2:15 MSG

Have you ever heard someone say, "Your actions are talking so loud that I can't hear what you're saying!" It's true—people pay much more attention to what you do than to what you say. That's why the way you live as a child of God is crucial. Those who would dismiss you as a religious fanatic when you try to talk to them about your relationship with your Creator will be unable to ignore your exemplary life. Let them see Jesus in you.

*When others look at me, I pray they see Jesus in my actions.
Lord, help me to love others with the love of Christ.*

Day 159

CATCHING FISH

No one has ever seen God; but if we love one another,
God lives in us and his love is made complete in us.
1 JOHN 4:12 NIV

It's hard to be a good witness if you have a sour expression on your face. People aren't usually won to the Lord by grumpy friends and coworkers. If you hope to persuade people that life in Jesus is the ultimate, then you have to let your enthusiasm shine through. Before you reach for the net, spend some time on your knees, asking for an infusion of joy. Then go catch some fish!

Father, fill me with the joy of Jesus so others might
recognize that there is something different about my
life and desire the very same for their own lives.

Day 160

GOD WILL ANSWER

*In the morning, LORD, you hear my voice; in the morning
I lay my requests before you and wait expectantly.*
PSALM 5:3 NIV

Hoping takes a lot of faith. Expecting takes even more. But you can do both when it comes to your faith and your prayers. It's not that you will always pray for a specific thing and get it, like placing a catalog order online (not that that always works out either). But what you can expect, when you lay your concerns before God, is that He will answer. Your prayers do not fall on disregarding ears. You can count on that.

*Your mercies are new every morning, Father.
Hear my cries to You. I know You are near.*

Day 161

A BEAUTIFUL AROMA

Since God chose you to be the holy people he loves,
you must clothe yourselves with tenderhearted mercy,
kindness, humility, gentleness, and patience.
COLOSSIANS 3:12 NLT

Have you ever noticed that we're naturally drawn to people who are fun to be around, people who radiate joy? They are like a garden of thornless roses: they put off a beautiful aroma and draw people quite naturally. If you want to win people to the Lord, then woo them with your kindness. Put off an inviting aroma. Win them with your love. Radiate joy!

May I win others for You, Lord, simply because they notice
a joy that radiates from within my spirit. Give me
opportunities to share that my joy is from You.

Day 162

PONDERING ETERNITY

And the ransomed of the LORD shall return, and come to Zion with songs and everlasting joy upon their heads: they shall obtain joy and gladness, and sorrow and sighing shall flee away.

ISAIAH 35:10 KJV

Have you pondered eternity? Forever and ever and ever. . .? Our finite minds can't grasp the concept, and yet one thing we understand from scripture: we will enter eternity in a state of everlasting joy and gladness. No more tears! No sorrow! An eternal joy-fest awaits us! Now that's something to celebrate!

While I can't imagine what heaven will really be like, Lord, I know it is a beautiful place. One day all things will be made right again. Until then, I long for my eternal home.

Day 163

HIS GLORIOUS RETURN

"Be ready all the time. For I, the Messiah,
will come when least expected."
LUKE 12:40 TLB

Jesus promised His return, and He asked that His followers watch for Him. He didn't tell us when—only that it will be when the world least expects Him. Only those who are sensitive to His Holy Spirit will recognize the times and the seasons. He expects you to live with the certainty that He will return soon, and to live your life accordingly. What a glorious day that will be. Look for it! Expect it!

I want to wait for Your return like a child waits for Christmas morning! Give me an expectant heart, Lord.

Day 164

BLESSING IN SECRET

*For they gave according to their means, as I can testify,
and beyond their means, of their own accord.*
2 Corinthians 8:3 ESV

Have you ever felt like giving just to bless someone? Just to bring joy to a friend's heart? Just to lift a burden? There's something rather exciting about giving in secret, isn't there? And when you reach way down deep—giving out of your own need—it's even more fun. Today, take inventory of the people in your life. Who can you bless in secret?

*Open my eyes to an opportunity, Father. Make a way for
me to be a blessing in secret to someone this week.*

Day 165
BE ALERT

Keep alert, stand firm in your faith, be courageous,
be strong. Let all that you do be done in love.
1 Corinthians 16:13–14 nrsv

Faith is not something you commit to once then don't think about again. Instead, it's something that alerts you every day to possibilities and opportunities. God has called you to live a life of vibrant faith, open to His direction, keeping your eyes on Him. Day by day you will see His faithfulness and your faith will grow. Soon you will stop worrying about what is around the next corner. You'll know with certainty that the two of you can handle any eventuality.

God, give me the strength and courage I need to face
every hardship that comes my way. I trust in You.

Day 166

CHANGE YOUR WORLD

*"But you will receive power when the Holy Spirit
has come upon you; and you shall be My witnesses
both in Jerusalem, and in all Judea and Samaria,
and even to the remotest part of the earth."*

ACTS 1:8 NASB

Want to experience real joy in your life? Then become a powerful witness. The most effective witness for Christ is one who is wholly surrendered to God's will and who has invited the Holy Spirit to do a transforming work in her life. After all, we can't really share the Good News if our lives haven't been truly changed. Allow the Lord to renovate you from the inside out—then change your world!

Father, may I be a witness for You in every action I take and every word I speak. I pray this in Jesus' name. Amen.

Day 167

HEART RENOVATION

Restore unto me the joy of thy salvation;
and uphold me with thy free spirit.
PSALM 51:12 KJV

When you restore your home, you return it to its prior state—its best possible condition. But is it possible to restore joy? Can you really get it back once its lost? Of course you can! Joy is a choice and can be restored with a single decision. Decide today. Make up your mind. Get ready for the renovation to take place as you ask the Lord to restore the joy of your salvation.

Today I choose joy. In the midst of trials and uncertainties,
I will trust in You, Lord. Fill my heart with joy!

Day 168

MULTIPLYING MERCY

Mercy unto you, and peace, and love, be multiplied.
JUDE 2 KJV

Have you ever done the math on God's mercy? If so, you've probably figured out that it just keeps multiplying itself out, over and over again. We mess up; He extends mercy. We mess up again; He pours out mercy once again. In the same way, peace, love, and joy are multiplied back to us. Praise the Lord! God's mathematics work in our favor.

God, Your mercy is amazing. Your grace abounds.
Thank You for not giving me what I deserve!

Day 169

LIVING BY FAITH

We live by faith, not by sight.
2 Corinthians 5:7 niv

You've probably heard it before: seeing isn't believing; believing is seeing. It's more than a twist on a phrase. Your faith opens you up to a new awareness of life around you. It enables you to see more from God's point of view. It reminds you that life is not just about the everyday realities but also mystery and possibilities. When you believe, you live according to a whole other reality with sights and sounds unimaginable to faithless eyes.

As I walk through this day, may I live by faith in You,
my sovereign God, even when I don't understand Your plan.

Day 170

ENTERING GOD'S PRESENCE TOGETHER

Saying, I will declare thy name unto my brethren, in the midst of the church will I sing praise unto thee.
HEBREWS 2:12 KJV

The most amazing thing happens when we gather together in our various churches. When we lift our voices in joyous praise to the Lord, something majestic occurs. In the very midst of our praise, God declares Himself to His people. He's there! The next time you gather together with fellow believers for a time of worship, pause a moment and reflect on the fact that you're entering into God's presence—together!

Thank You, Lord, that I am not alone. There will always be a remnant of Your people. We worship You in spirit and in truth.

Day 171

THE PROMISE
OF REWARD

The faithful will abound with blessings.
PROVERBS 28:20 NRSV

We've all had tasks that looked easy at the onset but later threatened to scuttle our resolve. We wonder if it's worth it to hang on. But when we do, we find that the reward of the task accomplished is even sweeter. Are you wondering if you can finish the task God has assigned to you? Don't give up. Your faithfulness to God's purposes holds the promise of great reward. Ask God to help you faithfully carry on until the job is done.

I will finish the task in your strength, O God. You have been so faithful to me. Find me faithful, Lord.

Day 172

UNFAILING FAITHFULNESS

Your love, LORD, reaches to the heavens,
your faithfulness to the skies.
PSALM 36:5 NIV

God won't abandon you. He won't walk away. His faithfulness reaches farther than you can see or even imagine. It's difficult to take in that kind of faithfulness when you live in a world full of disappointments. But if you can get quiet enough inside to sense God's never-changing presence and His steadfast commitment to you, you can survive the disappointments of this life so much more bravely. His faithfulness never fails!

When I gaze into the skies, they seem to go on forever,
just like Your faithfulness. Thank You, Lord.

Day 173

CHILDLIKE TRUST

For you have been my hope, Sovereign LORD,
my confidence since my youth.
PSALM 71:5 NIV

Remember how, as a child, you waited on pins and needles for Christmas to come? You hoped against hope that you would get those toys you asked for. You knew that good things were coming. That same level of expectation can motivate you as an adult. Your Father wants you to trust Him with childlike faith. Put your trust in Him, and watch how He moves on your behalf.

My trust is in You alone, Lord—not in this
world. Help me to have childlike faith.

Day 174

STOCKING THE VAULT

All thy children shall be taught of the Lord;
and great shall be the peace of thy children.
Isaiah 54:13 kjv

There's no heritage like the knowledge of God's love. There's no inheritance as empowering. As you live your life of faith before your family, it's like stocking a vault that will bless everyone. And it's never too late to begin. As you live authentically before God, you leave a blueprint for those who are watching. That example can last for generations beyond your view and be more influential than you can fathom.

Lord, help me to leave footprints worthy of following.
May future generations recognize You in my life,
and as a result, seek You for themselves.

Day 175

YOU ARE WITNESSES

The life appeared; we have seen it and testify to it,
and we proclaim to you the eternal life, which was
with the Father and has appeared to us.
1 John 1:2 niv

We don't have to work hard at being good witnesses when we're walking in close relationship with the Lord. Our witness will flow quite naturally out of our relationship with God. In other words, we *are* witnesses, simply by living the life He has called us to live. And by living the life, we point others toward eternal life. Now, that will cause joy to rise up in your soul!

Lord, I don't just want You to be part of my life—I want You to
be my whole life! May my life testify to Your glory! Amen.

Day 176

WOMANLY WISDOM

A wise woman strengthens her family.
PROVERBS 14:1 NCV

The influence of a woman on her family is phenomenal—for good and for bad. Sadly, some women weaken their families through selfishness, ambition, and carelessness. The vigilant, wise, and godly woman holds her family together, makes sacrifices to ensure its stability, and entreats God's blessing with her prayers. You can be that kind of woman—the kind that builds up and strengthens. Ask God to help you. He will show you how.

God, show me how to encourage and strengthen those around me. I want to be a godly influence on my family and friends.

Day 177

LIVING A BALANCED LIFE

Anything I wanted, I would take. I denied myself no pleasure. I even found great pleasure in hard work, a reward for all my labors.
ECCLESIASTES 2:10 NLT

Work beckons. Deadlines loom. You're trying to balance your home life against your work life, and it's overwhelming. Take heart! It is possible to rejoice in your labors—to find pleasure in the day-to-day tasks. At work or at play, let the Lord cause a song of joy to rise up in your heart.

May I find you in the day-to-day, Lord. You are present here and now. I want to recognize You in every moment.

Day 178

TENDING THE BODY OF CHRIST

*So we, being many, are one body in Christ,
and every one members one of another.*
ROMANS 12:5 KJV

There's a lot of work to be done in the local church. Someone has to teach the children, vacuum the floors, prepare meals for the sick, and so forth. With so many needs, how does the body of Christ function without its various members feeling taken advantage of? If you're in a position of service at your local church, praise God for the opportunity to serve others. Step out—with joy leading the way.

Father, remind me that my volunteering isn't something that just needs checked off my to-do list; it's an opportunity to serve others with a joyful heart!

Day 179

FAVORED CHILD

May those who delight in my vindication shout for joy and
gladness; may they always say, "The LORD be exalted,
who delights in the well-being of his servant."
PSALM 35:27 NIV

Do you ever feel like God's favorite child? Ever marvel at the fact
that He continues to bestow His extraordinary favor upon you,
even when you don't deserve it? God takes great pleasure in
you and wants to bless you above all you could ask or think. So,
when you're in a season of favor, praise Him. Shout for joy and
be glad! Tell others about the great things the Lord has done.

Father, You have done great things in my life.
I will always testify to Your goodness and glory.

Day 180

EMOTIONAL EFFECTIVENESS

We can be sure when we say, "I will not be afraid, because the Lord is my helper."
HEBREWS 13:6 NCV

Women are complex beings. Our emotions are our greatest strength, but they can also be the most unstable aspect of our character. How do you respond to the pressures and pleasures around you each day? Do you find yourself too emotional? God doesn't want to stifle your emotions—they allow you to feel His love, His compassion, His joy. Instead, He wants to help you harness them and use them for His kingdom. Will you let Him?

God, use every part of me—even these crazy emotions—for Your kingdom work, I pray.

Day 181

TRUSTING THROUGH THE STORM

When times are good, be happy; but when times are bad, consider this: God has made the one as well as the other.
ECCLESIASTES 7:14 NIV

You may tend to think of God gratefully in the good times and ask for His help in the bad. But sometimes you have to consider that God brings good out of both. No matter what your feelings tell you, you can trust Him to work out His purpose in you at all times. He isn't bound by your feelings. He is bound by His Word. You should not be bound by your feelings either but by His promises!

Lord, I will trust You in the good times and in the bad because You are good—all the time!

Day 182

THE FOUNTAIN OF SALVATION

With joy you will drink deeply from the fountain of salvation!
ISAIAH 12:3 NLT

In biblical times, women would go to the local well for water. They would drop the bucket down, down, down, then lift it up, filled to the brim. Today the Lord wants you to reach down into His well of salvation and, with great joy, draw up the bucket. Remember how He saved you? Delivered you? Remember His grace? Is your bucket filled to the brim? If so, then that's something to celebrate!

Lord, I celebrate because I have been given living water. I will never be thirsty again!

Day 183

THE SPIRITUAL COMMUNITY

*If we are living in the light of God's presence, just as Christ does,
then we have wonderful fellowship and joy with each other.*
1 JOHN 1:7 TLB

Living in close relationship with God empowers you to connect with people meaningfully. As you grow toward Him, you will find yourself growing in your relationships with others as well. It's the result of having the same heavenly Father, living in the same kingdom, and sharing the same destination—heaven. Enjoy the great spiritual family God has placed you in. It's the family of faith. Be there for them and let them be there for you. It's what God intended.

*Thank You, Lord, for my Christian community.
May I treat each member as family, for we
are brothers and sisters in Christ.*

Day 184

AWESTRUCK

His lord said unto him, Well done, thou good and faithful servant: thou hast been faithful over a few things, I will make thee ruler over many things: enter thou into the joy of thy lord.

MATTHEW 25:21 KJV

When you think of standing before the Lord—face-to-face—are you overwhelmed with fear or awestruck with great joy? Oh, what a glorious day it will be when we hear Him speak those words, "Well done, thou good and faithful servant." When He ushers us into the joy of His presence for all eternity, our fears and hesitations will be forever washed away. Spend time in joyous rehearsal today!

May my life honor You so that one day I may stand before You and You will recognize me as a faithful servant, Lord.

Day 185

THE FAMILY OF GOD

All of you should be in agreement, understanding each other,
loving each other as family, being kind and humble.

1 PETER 3:8 NCV

The family of God is in many respects like your natural family. You love them profoundly, but very often they can make you throw up your hands in frustration. Just like you, they all have those little areas where they are still growing and learning and becoming better people. When conflicts come, don't turn and run! It's important to work it out and see it through—for your Father's sake.

Lord, help me to be patient with people who frustrate me.
Remind me to show them grace as You have
shown mercy in my life.

Day 186

FISCAL RESPONSIBILITY

*Wealth hastily gotten will dwindle, but those
who gather little by little will increase it.*
PROVERBS 13:11 NRSV

In a world where people win lotteries and game shows to suddenly come into a lot of cash, it's easy to wonder if it's worth it to put that little bit into savings each paycheck. The Bible says a lot about money, though, and affirms that it is the wise person who builds that nest egg as they can, a little at a time along the way. Besides the investment, that bit you put away, no matter how small, is a vote for your future.

*Help me to be wise with money, Lord. Give me
insight to know how to save and spend, I pray.*

Day 187

MORNING DEW

The faithful love of the LORD never ends! His mercies never cease.
Great is his faithfulness; his mercies begin afresh each morning.
LAMENTATIONS 3:22–23 NLT

Don't you love the newness of morning—the dew on the grass, the awakening sun, the quiet stillness of the day, when you can spend time alone with the Lord in solitude? Oh, what joy rises in our souls as we realize that God's love and mercy are new every morning! Each day is a fresh start, a new chance. Grace washes over us afresh, like the morning dew. Great is His faithfulness!

Thank You, Father, that each day is an opportunity for a
fresh new start. Wipe away the mistakes and messes
of yesterday, I pray. In Jesus' name, amen.

Day 188

JOYOUS PERSPECTIVE

*Let us draw near to God with a sincere heart and
with the full assurance that faith brings.*
HEBREWS 10:22 NIV

Ever looked through a pair of binoculars? What if you peered through the lenses and caught a glimpse of God's face? What if you could see things the way He sees them? Hear things the way He hears them? What an amazing perspective! Every time you draw near to God, He offers you the opportunity to see Him. To find Him. To trust Him. Let Him give you His joyous perspective today.

*May I see the world through a God-lens.
Please grant me Your perspective on the people
around me and on the events of this day.*

Day 189

GODLY SAVINGS

*My God will meet all your needs according
to the riches of his glory in Christ Jesus.*
PHILIPPIANS 4:19 NIV

It may seem strange to learn that God cares about money. While He isn't subject to it, He knows that you are—while you live in this world at least. The Bible provides good advice about staying out of debt, saving all you can, being generous with others, and giving to the support of God's work. These habits put you in line for God's blessings. He describes them as "running over" and invites you to test Him and see.

*Help me, Lord, to live debt-free so I might
be abundantly generous with others.*

Day 190

A LIFETIME OF BLESSING

*For his anger lasts only a moment, but his
favor lasts a lifetime; weeping may stay for
the night, but rejoicing comes in the morning.*

Psalm 30:5 NIV

Can you picture a lifetime of blessing? Hard to imagine, isn't it?
We think of "seasons" of blessing, but God continually pours
out His favor upon His children. We have our ups and downs—
our sorrows and our joys—but God remains consistent, never
changing. We weep in the bad times and celebrate during the
good. Oh, if only we could remember that on the tail end of
every sorrow, there is a joyful tomorrow!

*There is always joy to be found in You, Lord.
Help me cling to the hope of tomorrow.*

Day 191

BLESSED FORGIVENESS

"I forgive you all that you have done," says the Lord God.
EZEKIEL 16:63 TLB

You are forgiven. No matter what you've done. No matter how or when or what—God's forgiveness is waiting for you. The moment you acknowledge your sin and ask to be forgiven, it's done. Strangely, that may be difficult for you to accept. You may feel you must make your own atonement. But it's a feat you will never accomplish. Only God's perfect Son was able to do the job. Abandon your pride and receive His forgiveness. Don't wait another moment.

Thank You for forgiveness, Lord. It is undeserved, but I am so thankful that You pour it out freely when I ask.

Day 192

CHANGING SEASONS

*To every thing there is a season, and a time
to every purpose under the heaven.*
ECCLESIASTES 3:1 KJV

Oh, those changing seasons! We watch in wonder as the vibrant green leaves slowly morph into dry brown ones, eventually losing their grip on the trees and drifting down to the ground below. Change is never easy, particularly when you have to let go of the past. But oh, the joy of recognizing that God sees into the future. He knows that springtime is coming. Our best days are ahead!

*I love to watch the seasons change, Lord.
Help me to trust You in every season of my life.*

Day 193

WALKING STREETS OF GOLD

I saw the Lord sitting upon his throne, and all the host of heaven standing on his right hand and on his left.
2 Chronicles 18:18 KJV

What do you think of when you ponder the word *heaven*? What will it be like to walk on streets of gold, to see our loved ones who have gone before us? How thrilling to know we will one day meet our Lord and Savior face-to-face. He has gone to prepare a place for us—and what a place it will be! The joy of eternity is ours as believers. Praise Him!

Thank You, Abba Father. I know that one day, in heaven, You will make all things right. I wait expectantly for that day.

Day 194

THE PRIVILEGE
OF FORGIVENESS

*Bear with one another and, if anyone has a complaint
against another, forgive each other; just as the
Lord has forgiven you, so you also must forgive.*
COLOSSIANS 3:13 NRSV

If you've ever tried to forgive another person, even a close
friend or family member, you know how difficult that can be.
Everything in you wants to cling to the hurt and publish the
offense. God invites you to forgive out of gratitude for what He
has done for you. He has forgiven you—freely and completely.
Remember that no one could hurt you as much as your sin
has hurt your heavenly Father. When you look at it that way,
forgiveness becomes a privilege.

*Help me forgive as You forgive, Father. May I find it an
honor to dismiss another's sin toward me, I pray.*

Day 195

HEAVENLY PERSPECTIVE

*Yea, all kings shall fall down before
him: all nations shall serve him.*
PSALM 72:11 KJV

There's coming a day when every knee will bow and every
tongue confess that Jesus Christ is Lord. Does it seem impossible
right now, in light of current world events? If only we could
see things the way God does! He knows that the kings of the
nations will one day fall down before Him. Oh, what a glorious
and joyful day that will be!

*The whole world does not worship You, heavenly
Father, but one day every knee shall bow. Your
truth and righteousness will prevail.*

Day 196

FREE AT LAST

The Lord sets prisoners free.
PSALM 146:7 NIV

Some women run from God, thinking He will ask them to surrender their freedom and lock them down to some religious regimen. In reality, just the opposite is true. We are all already in bondage to our unwashed thoughts and behaviors and our sinful nature. Before you can flourish in God's kingdom, He has to remove your bonds. Fortunately, your heavenly Father is in the chain-breaking business. Ask Him to set you free.

Thank You for the chains You have broken in my life, Lord. I will leave them in the past, never to be weighed down by them again.

Day 197

CULTIVATING A MERRY HEART

Go, eat your food with gladness, and drink your wine with a joyful heart, for God has already approved what you do.
ECCLESIASTES 9:7 NIV

Ever feel like nothing you do is good enough? Your boss is frustrated over something you've done wrong. The kids are complaining. Your neighbors are even upset at you. How wonderful to read that God accepts our works, even when we feel lacking. He encourages us to go our way with a merry heart, completely confident that we are accepted in the Beloved.

I am so thankful that I am always enough for You. I am accepted and forever cherished by my Father. I love You, Lord. Amen.

Day 198

THE ROCK OF OUR SALVATION

*O come, let us sing unto the Lord: let us make
a joyful noise to the rock of our salvation.*
Psalm 95:1 kjv

God never changes. He is the same—yesterday, today, and forever. We go through a multitude of changes in our lives, but, praise God, He is consistent. Doesn't that bring joy to your heart, to realize that the Creator of the universe is our Rock? And don't you feel like celebrating when you realize that, no matter how much you mess up, His promise of salvation is true? Praise be to the Lord, our Rock!

*You are my Rock, Lord. I will glorify You! When
everything around me is unpredictable and
unstable, You are steadfast and true.*

Day 199

JUSTIFIED BY GRACE

That being justified by his grace, we should be made
heirs according to the hope of eternal life.
TITUS 3:7 KJV

Have you ever been the recipient of an inheritance? Ever had
a family member pass away, leaving you money or objects?
There is an inheritance that far exceeds anything we could ever
receive in this world. By God's grace, we are His heirs! What do
we inherit? Eternal life! If you haven't already done so, place
your trust in Christ today and experience the joy of becoming
His child. Oh, the joy of a godly inheritance!

Because of Your grace, God, I am part of Your family
and have inherited abundant, eternal life.

Day 200

PASSION AND PURPOSE

In Him also we have obtained an inheritance, being
predestined according to the purpose of Him who
works all things according to the counsel of His will.
EPHESIANS 1:11 NKJV

Father, I'm in a rut. I like some familiarity, but this monotony is wearing away at my sense of purpose. I know there are parts of our lives that are not particularly glamorous, fulfilling, or significant (at least on the surface). Yet living without passion or purpose isn't what You had in mind for us. Show me, Lord, how to find meaning in my everyday life. Help me to see the subtle nuances of joy folded into life's mundane hours. I put my longings into Your hands. Amen.

May I discover hope in the humble and passion
in the plain. All things work together for
my good because I love You, Lord.

Day 201

THE WORK OF
YOUR HANDS

*May the favor of the Lord our God rest on us; establish the work
of our hands for us—yes, establish the work of our hands.*
PSALM 90:17 NIV

It's interesting to think of "favor" and "the work of our hands"
in the same sentence, isn't it? In God's economy, favor equals
usefulness. We want the work of our hands to make a difference
in this world, and we want to see God smiling down on our
ventures. Today, ask God to establish the work of your hands.
Then watch as His favor rests upon you!

*Lord, work through me in this world.
Use me. May Your favor be upon my life.*

Day 202

FREEDOM IN THE SPIRIT

The Lord is the Spirit, and where the
Spirit of the Lord is, there is freedom.
2 CORINTHIANS 3:17 NIV

Wherever the Spirit of God goes, freedom follows. If His Spirit dwells in you, you will experience more freedom than you have ever known. You will no longer be inhibited by selfishness and resentment. You will be free to do what you were created to do—live in right relationship with your Creator. Don't struggle to free yourself. You haven't the power or the strength. Invite God's Holy Spirit to come inside your heart and free you in the process.

Holy Spirit, have Your way in my heart. Guide me. Comfort
me. Reveal the will of God to me, I pray. Amen.

Day 203

THE DESIRES OF
YOUR HEART

*Delight yourself in the LORD, and he will
give you the desires of your heart.*
PSALM 37:4 ESV

What are the deepest desires of your heart? Ponder that question a moment. If you could really do—or have—what you longed for, what would that be? The key to receiving from the Lord is delighting in Him. Draw near. Spend time with your head against His shoulder, feeling His heartbeat. Ask that your requests come into alignment with His will. Then, with utmost joy, make your petitions known.

*Lord, my delight is in You, and I will
serve You all the days of my life.*

Day 204

LIVING A NEW LIFE

You have begun to live the new life, in which you are being made new and are becoming like the One who made you.
COLOSSIANS 3:10 NCV

God's work in your life doesn't simply make you a better person; it makes you more like Him! That's really true of any loving relationship—the more you focus on another person and interact with him or her, the more you pick up that person's habits and interests. In the same way—but even more because of the work of the Spirit—as you focus on God and interact with Him, His nature is recovered in your life.

You are the Creator and I am the created, Lord, and I am so thankful to be made in Your image. Thank You for new life.

Day 205

TAKING THE
RIGHT PATH

*What do people get for all the toil and anxious
striving with which they labor under the sun?*
ECCLESIASTES 2:22 NIV

Imagine you're approaching a fork in the road. You're unsure of
which way to turn. If you knew ahead of time that the road to
the right would be filled with joy and the road to left would lead
to sorrow, wouldn't it make the decision easier? Today, as you
face multiple decisions, ask God to lead you down the right road.

Lord, wherever You lead, I will follow. Amen.

Day 206

TRUE FRIENDS

A friend loves at all times.
They are there to help when trouble comes.
PROVERBS 17:17 NIrV

Tough times reveal real friends. Partly that is true because real friends are the ones that stick around when things are troublesome and uncomfortable and not at all fun. But also it is true because when you are at your worst or weakest, you can only bear to be witnessed by real friends—those who already know you inside and out and accept you just the way you are. Ask God to give you that kind of friend.

Lord, show me the friends that I should allow to be in
my closest circle. You walked closest with the Twelve.
May I be blessed with a few close Christian friends.

Day 207

AUTHENTIC FRIENDSHIP

Some friends play at friendship but a true friend sticks closer than one's nearest kin.
PROVERBS 18:24 NRSV

It's nice to have acquaintances. But somewhere within us, we crave authentic friendships that provide a connection as strong as that of our biological families. Do you have friendships that reach to this level? If not, ask God to help you find the ones that you can go deeper with. Then keep your eyes and ears open. Reach out to others, and let God do the rest. He won't disappoint you.

God, thank You for friends. Please bless me with a few Christ followers with whom I can go deep in this life.

Day 208

FIX YOUR EYES
ON JESUS

*Fixing our eyes on Jesus, the pioneer and
perfecter of faith. For the joy set before him
he endured the cross, scorning its shame, and sat
down at the right hand of the throne of God.*
HEBREWS 12:2 NIV

Jesus walked through many seasons in His ministry here on
earth. He walked through seasons of great favor, when crowds
flocked to Him and when voices cried out, "Blessed is He who
comes in the name of the Lord!" But He also walked through
seasons of ultimate rejection as He headed up Golgotha's hill.
We will go through good times and bad, but, like Jesus, we can
say, "But for the joy set before me, I will endure."

*Help me to turn my eyes upon Jesus and look full in
His wonderful face all the days of my life. Amen.*

Day 209

ABIDE IN HIM

[Jesus said,] "Abide in me as I abide in you. Just as the branch cannot bear fruit by itself unless it abides in the vine, neither can you unless you abide in me."
JOHN 15:4 NRSV

You may think you aren't accomplishing anything in your life. Perhaps you work at a dead-end job or a disability has left you feeling useless and alone. No matter what your circumstances, God has a plan for you, and that plan is not out of reach. As long as you are looking to Him, your life will be fruitful and fulfilling. That's His will, His promise, and His plan.

God, please reveal Your will to me as
I live my life day by day for You. Amen.

Day 210

BROKEN PROMISES

And this is what he promised us—eternal life.
1 John 2:25 niv

Ever had a friend or loved one make a promise, only to break it? What about you? Ever broken a promise? We all fail in this area, don't we? Thankfully, God is not a promise breaker. When He promised you would spend eternity with Him if you accepted the work of His Son on the cross, He meant it. Doesn't it bring joy to your heart to know God won't break His promises?

Promise Keeper, I am so thankful that You never let me down. You are the same yesterday, today, and forever. You keep Your promises to Your children.

Day 211

YOU ARE CHOSEN

"You did not choose me, but I chose you and appointed you so that you might go and bear fruit—fruit that will last."
JOHN 15:16 NIV

Have you looked at yourself and thought, *God could never use me*? You've decided that you aren't worthy to go out in His name, to speak on His behalf, to carry His message, to fulfill His plan. If it were up to you, you wouldn't appoint yourself to do anything. But it isn't up to you. God does the choosing, and He wants to use you. He has given you a job to do. Open your heart and mind to Him, and much fruit will follow.

God, I am not the smartest or the strongest, but all that I am I give to You. Use me for Your glory. In Jesus' name, amen.

Day 212

THE FRUIT OF
YOUR LABOR

*You will eat the fruit of your labor; blessings
and prosperity will be yours.*
PSALM 128:2 NIV

We're always waiting for the payoff, aren't we? When we've put a lot of effort into a project, for example, we hope to see good results. The Word of God promises that we will eat the fruit of our labor—that we will eventually experience blessings and prosperity. So all of that hard work will be worth it. But remember, the joy is in the journey! It's not just in the payoff.

*Thank You, Lord, that the fruit of my labor will pay
off in the end. Help me to focus on the rewards
found in daily life as I walk with You.*

Day 213
JOY OUT OF SORROW

They that sow in tears shall reap in joy.
PSALM 126:5 KJV

Periods of great sorrow are unavoidable. Perhaps the death of a loved one has left you floundering. Or maybe your heart has been broken by someone you thought you could trust. If you've been through an earthshaking change—one you weren't expecting or feel you didn't deserve—then turn to the One who can replenish you. God will walk with you through this valley and promises to replace your tears with joy.

God, I know that one day there will be no more tears. Until then, please comfort me in sorrow.

Day 214

SINGING UNTO ZION

Therefore the redeemed of the LORD shall return, and
come with singing unto Zion; and everlasting joy shall
be upon their head: they shall obtain gladness and joy;
and sorrow and mourning shall flee away.
ISAIAH 51:11 KJV

God longs for people across the globe to turn their hearts to Him. He wants them to understand that He sent His only begotten Son to earth to die on a rugged cross so that people of every ethnicity could be set free from their sins. Oh, that people around the world would turn to God, would return to Him with singing and with everlasting joy upon their heads!

Lord, may the world turn to You. You are the
Light in the darkness and our only hope. Amen.

Day 215

OVERCOMING FAMILIAL OBSTACLES

*Now the God of hope fill you with all joy and
peace in believing, that ye may abound in
hope, through the power of the Holy Ghost.*
ROMANS 15:13 KJV

Living in a family environment isn't always easy. Siblings bicker.
Tempers flare. People get their feelings hurt. If you want to
experience joy in your family, then ask the Lord to give you
hope, especially when things are going wrong. Through the
power of the Holy Spirit, you can overcome those obstacles,
but you have to address them head-on. Today, make a list of
problems you're facing, then ask for God's input.

*God of hope, fill me with joy and peace, I pray. I believe
in You and the power of the Holy Spirit who lives in me.*

Day 216

HIS PLAN FOR YOU

I know the plans I have for you, says the Lord, plans for your welfare and not for harm, to give you a future with hope.
JEREMIAH 29:11 NRSV

Your age doesn't matter. Your looks don't matter. Your circumstances don't matter. For every individual, every life, God has a plan for the future. Even if you are reading this book from a hospital bed from which you never expect to leave, God has given you a future. Don't drop out of life for any reason. With Him, your best days are yet to come—better than you can think or imagine.

Giver of life, Your plans are always right for Your children. As I follow hard after You, You will use everything in my life for good. Amen.

NAVIGATING PHASES

*"I will make them and the places surrounding
my hill a blessing. I will send down showers
in season; there will be showers of blessing."*
EZEKIEL 34:26 NIV

How do we shift from one project to the next? One phase of life
to the next? We can move forward with joy leading the way when
we realize that God is the giver of the seasons. He designed them
and showers us with blessings as we move through each one,
even the tough ones. Good news! Change is always just around
the bend. Oh, the joy of knowing the hard times won't last!

*God, You are always with me. Thank You for the
blessings You surprise me with in every stage of life.*

Day 218

JOY IN THE FUTURE

Do not be conformed to this world, but be transformed by the renewing of your mind.

ROMANS 12:2 NKJV

Do you ever find yourself worrying about tomorrow? Not sure of what it will bring? Oh, what hope lies in the unseen tomorrow! What unexpected joys are just around the corner. Sure, you can't see them, but they're there! Before you give in to fear, allow the Lord to transform your mind. See tomorrow as He sees it—filled with unexpected joys.

Lord, please clean house in my heart.
Fill me up with You. Renew my mind, I pray.

Day 219

ENDLESS POSSIBILITIES

Good people can look forward to a bright future.
PROVERBS 13:9 NCV

When your life is hid in the goodness of God, your possibilities are limitless. Your future is more than bright—it's dazzling. If you are at the beginning of your walk with God, you are a fortunate woman. The road ahead may not be easy, but it will be the greatest adventure, the greatest race you've ever attempted. And best of all, the destination is certain. Throw yourself unreservedly into the work that God has called you to. Take hold of your future with both hands.

God, thank You that my future is bright because my righteousness is found in Christ alone. You have good plans for me!

Day 220

THE QUIET CALL
TO REPENTANCE

*"Take my yoke upon you, and learn from me;
for I am gentle and humble in heart,
and you will find rest for your souls."*
MATTHEW 11:29 NRSV

God could blast you for your sinfulness. He could reprimand you every time you stumble and chastise you for every mistake you make. He will correct you, of course. How else can He keep you on the right path? But God's correction is consistently gentle. No throwing of lightning bolts and crashing thunderclaps, just a still, small voice inside your heart. He will not make an excuse for your sin, but He will quietly and gently call you to repentance.

*Lord, thank You that I no longer have to bear the
heavy load of my sin. You have forgiven me,
and You have carried the weight for me!*

Day 221

EVIDENT GENTLENESS

Let your gentleness be evident to all.
The Lord is near.

Philippians 4:5 niv

The Bible says that the strong woman is also gentle—two words that might seem contradictory. But they aren't. The strong woman chooses how she will respond to others. She chooses to deal with them gently—because she can. She is in control of her emotions, her words, and her actions. Anger, hostility—both represent the easy way out. But gentleness requires strength. God wants to see you become a strong, gentle woman for Him.

Lord, I find it hard to be gentle at times. Calm my
spirit, and help me to control my tongue, I pray.

Day 222

THE FRUIT OF
THE SPIRIT

But the fruit of the Spirit is love, joy, peace,
longsuffering, gentleness, goodness, faith.
GALATIANS 5:22 KJV

Want to know how to have the ideal family environment? Want to see parents living in peace with teens? To obtain a joyous family environment, you have to have a fruit-bowl mentality. Dealing with anger? Reach inside the bowl for peace. Struggling with impatience? Grab a slice of long-suffering. Having a problem with depression? Reach for joy. Keep that fruit bowl close by! It's going to come in handy!

Lord, may the fruit of the Spirit be evident in my life to all
those around me—especially those with whom I live and work.
Sometimes it is the hardest to show love to those closest to me.

Day 223

THE WAY
OF GOODNESS

When wisdom enters your heart, and knowledge is pleasant
to your soul. . .you may walk in the way of goodness.
PROVERBS 2:10, 20 NKJV

When you were a little girl, your parents may have said, "Run along now and be a good little girl." They meant only the best, but growing up, many women received a negative message. They relate goodness to being dismissed or not being taken seriously. Others become obsessed with meeting an unrealistic standard of goodness. Really no one is good but God. Goodness will come as you walk in relationship with Him.

My goodness is found in You, Lord. My righteousness
is only through Your Son. Amen.

Day 224

JOY IN GOOD DEEDS

As we have opportunity, let us do good to all people,
especially to those who belong to the family of believers.
GALATIANS 6:10 NIV

Good deeds are an expression of the goodness or "God-ness" that resides within you. They should come easily, naturally. As you feel God's presence within and see Him moving in your affairs, as you feel your heart flooding with gratitude for what He has done for you, reach out to others. Let them feel the overflow of God's goodness to you. Good deeds aren't something you force yourself to do. They are the joyous privilege of the child of God.

God, I know it is a great responsibility to pray for
opportunities to do good, because when You show them
to me, I must act. Please give me these opportunities.

Day 225

FAVOR IN GOD'S EYES

But Noah found favor in the eyes of the LORD.
GENESIS 6:8 NIV

Ever wonder why Noah stood out head and shoulders above others in his generation? Why did God look upon him with favor? Noah walked with God and was righteous. Do you have what it takes to be a "Noah" in this generation? Walk with God daily. Don't let the things of this world zap your strength. Trust Him, live for Him, and watch Him rain down favor in your life!

God, make me a modern-day Noah. May I be found faithful and true to You as I walk through life with You day by day.

Day 226

GOD'S UNMERITED FAVOR

By the grace of God I am what I am, and his grace to me
was not without effect. No, I worked harder than all of
them—yet not I, but the grace of God that was with me.
1 Corinthians 15:10 NIV

Grace is often defined as God's unmerited favor. It means that His love for us, His care, and His concern are all free gifts; we haven't earned them. What a wonderful thing to be loved and accepted—just because! In God's eyes, you are already pretty enough, smart enough, well enough to receive His best. He loves you for yourself. He wants you to become all you were created to be, but your relationship with Him doesn't hinge on it. What a wonderful word grace is!

Your grace, Father, is greater than all my sin.
Thank You, Father God, for unmerited favor.

Day 227
ALL THE NATIONS

All of you nations, come praise the LORD! Let everyone praise him.
PSALM 117:1 CEV

Can you imagine the sound of millions of people singing praises to the Lord in thousands of different languages simultaneously? On any given day, God hears people all over the world lift up their praises to Him in their native tongues. Oh, what a joyful sound that must be to our heavenly Father. Today, as you lift your voice, think of the millions of others who join you. Praise Him! Oh, praise Him!

Father God, sometimes I forget that people praise You in every language! What a beautiful sound that must be to You. I praise You with every fiber of my being.

Day 228

GRACE TO THE HUMBLE

[God] shows favor to the humble.
PROVERBS 3:34 NIV

For many people, it's difficult to receive what they don't feel they have earned. Whether it's a sense of independence or pride, such an attitude will rob you of the best this life has to offer. You must be able to receive God's love, even when you don't feel lovable, and God's goodness, even when you don't feel deserving. God has freely given you everything—His kingdom! Don't stand on the sidelines whispering, "I'm not worthy." Humble yourself and receive.

I receive Your love, God. I accept it with my whole heart. I could never work enough or be good enough to earn it, but I accept it as a free gift.

Day 229

A SPIRITUALLY HEALTHY FAMILY

*I have no greater joy than to hear that
my children are walking in the truth.*
3 JOHN 4 NIV

God rejoices in a strong family. To maintain healthiness, it's important to examine where you all stand—as individuals—in your relationship with the Lord. Sometimes we focus on our own spiritual lives but don't pay much attention to where our children are. Today, ask the Lord to show you what you can do to help your children grow in the Lord. As they grow, so will your joy. And so will the Lord's!

*Lord, may the children in my life who look to me as an example
find me faithful to You. May they walk in truth all their days.*

Day 230

SEEKING GOD

Your ears shall hear a word behind you, saying, "This is the way, walk in it," whenever you turn to the right hand or whenever you turn to the left.

ISAIAH 30:21 NKJV

When we need answers, we often say we are "seeking God." And yet we need not seek Him since He is ever near. Nor are we seeking answers from God, for He has already given us the answers we need. Instead, we are seeking to hear those answers, to tune out the busy thoughts and preconceived notions we carry with us. If you need answers, ask God to help you listen and discern, to open your ears to hear His voice that was there all along.

God, give me ears to hear Your voice. You are my Good Shepherd. Tune my ears to know and follow Your voice.

Day 231

THE EYE OF GOD

*I will instruct you and teach you in the way
you should go; I will guide you with My eye.*
PSALM 32:8 NKJV

Have you been asking God for guidance, but the way before you is still unclear? It could be that you're expecting a full-blown road map—and God rarely answers that way. Instead, He gives the first step, and when you have taken that step, He reveals the next. That's how He encourages your faith and keeps you close to the path. It's enough really to know that He sees the path ahead. Trust Him!

*Father in heaven, please show me the way I should go—
day by day, hour by hour, moment by moment. Amen.*

Day 232

JOY DESPITE THE NEWS

*And they left the tomb quickly with fear and
great joy and ran to report it to His disciples.*
MATTHEW 28:8 NASB

Ever had a day when all of the news was good? You picked up the phone—good news. Read an email message—good news. Then, the very next day, all of the news was bad! How do we make sense of it all? Even those closest to Jesus went through ups and downs. One moment they mourned His death, and the next they celebrated His resurrection. Whether the news is good or bad, choose joy.

*Lord, I will choose joy on the best of days and on the worst.
In You there is always a reason to celebrate. Amen.*

Day 233

HAPPINESS VS. JOY

A happy heart makes the face cheerful,
but heartache crushes the spirit.
PROVERBS 15:13 NIV

Happiness is elusive in this life. Because it's an emotion—like sadness and anger—it comes and goes with the circumstances. Joy is different. It's the permanent condition of the heart that is right with God. It isn't based on circumstances, but rather the known outcome—eternity with God. Forget about the pursuit of happiness and embrace joy. It will not fail you even in your darkest days and most trying hours. Rejoice!

Even in the darkness, I can trust what I have seen
in the light. I choose joy in every circumstance
because You are always with me, Father God.

Day 234

FEELING LEFT OUT

*No one from the east or the west or from the desert
can exalt themselves. It is God who judges:
He brings one down, he exalts another.*
PSALM 75:6–7 NIV

Sometimes we grumble when others are exalted. We feel left out. Why do others prosper when everything around us seems to be falling apart? We can't celebrate their victories. We aren't joyful for them. Shame on us! God chooses whom to exalt—and when. We can't pretend to know His thoughts. But we can submit to His will and celebrate with those who are walking through seasons of great favor.

*Lord, please give me what it takes to celebrate with
others, even when I don't understand Your ways.*

Day 235

A RIGHT RELATIONSHIP WITH GOD

*May the righteous be glad and rejoice before
God; may they be happy and joyful.*
PSALM 68:3 NIV

Many women believe that happiness is a result of success. "When I find the right person to marry, I'll be happy." "When I achieve my career goals...." "When I can afford the home I really want...." The truth is that real happiness—deep inner joy—is the result of living in right relationship with God rather than the trappings of success. Regardless of what you may be facing—good and bad—be happy knowing you are pleasing your heavenly Father.

God, I find great contentment in being Your daughter. Help me to live day by day with You at the center of my life.

Day 236

TEARS OF JOY

*Break forth into joy, sing together, you waste
places of Jerusalem! For the LORD has comforted
His people, He has redeemed Jerusalem.*

ISAIAH 52:9 NKJV

Have you ever knelt to comfort a child as the tears flowed down his or her little cheeks? If so, then you understand the heart of your Daddy God as He gently wipes away your tears during times of sorrow. He comforts as only a Father can, bringing hope where there is no hope and joy where there is no joy. What a compassionate God we serve!

*God, thank You for being my Abba Father, my Daddy.
You comfort me like no one else can. Amen.*

Day 237

GOD'S MARVELOUS CREATION

Let the floods clap their hands: let the hills be joyful together.
Psalm 98:8 KJV

All of nature sings the praises of our mighty God. Look around you! Do you see the hills off in the distance, pointing up in majesty? Can you hear the water in the brooks, tumbling along in a chorus of praise? And what about the ocean waves? Oh, the joy in discovering the God of the universe through His marvelous creation!

May I worship You with all of creation, oh holy and perfect God of the universe. You are the one true God, and I will sing Your praises.

Day 238

OUR REFUGE AND STRENGTH

God is our refuge and strength, an ever-present help in trouble.
PSALM 46:1 NIV

Have you ever gone through a trial or heartache so painful that you couldn't even put it into words? It felt like a long, piercing scream was ripping you apart inside. Any number of things could cause such suffering—loss, divorce, betrayal, sickness. If you find yourself in such a place in your life, reach out to the Lord. He understands suffering at its deepest level. He knows how to comfort you. All you have to do is ask.

God, You are my hiding place and my refuge. When I call out to You for help, You come running to Your daughter with outstretched arms.

Day 239

PRAISE IN PUBLIC

And at midnight Paul and Silas prayed, and sang
praises unto God: and the prisoners heard them.
ACTS 16:25 KJV

Are you a closet praiser? Happy to worship God in the privacy of your own home but nervous about opening up and praising Him in public? Oh, may this be the day you break through that barrier. Corporate praise—coming together with your brothers and sisters in the Lord to worship Him—is powerful! May you come to know the fullness of His joy as you worship side by side with fellow believers!

God, may I never be ashamed to sing Your praise
and to lift my voice in prayer to You. There is
such power in praying with other believers!

Day 240

JOYFUL FAMILIES

"There you shall eat before the LORD your God, and you shall rejoice in all to which you have put your hand, you and your households, in which the LORD your God has blessed you."

DEUTERONOMY 12:7 NKJV

Did you grow up in a family where laughter was a key ingredient? Whether you grew up in a joyful home or not, it's surely your desire for the family you now have (or may one day have). God desires that your children walk in joy—and that starts with you. Children are, after all, a reflection of their parents. Today, throw open the windows of your home to the possibility of everlasting joy!

Father, may my home be a place of peace and joy, a refuge and haven for my family and for all who enter this place.

Day 241

OUR HELP AND SHIELD

Our soul waits for the LORD; He is our help and our shield.
PSALM 33:20 NKJV

Who do you turn to when trouble comes your way? You're blessed if you have faithful friends and loved ones here on earth. But whether you have such support in your life or not, God has promised that you will never face adversity alone. Again and again in the Bible, He declares His desire to help you. Even when no one else is there, He will be. And He has limitless resources. No matter what your need, call on Him.

God, I am never alone. You are always with me, and You promise never to forsake me. I find great comfort in that.

Day 242

AMAZING LOVE

He remembered his Covenant with them, and, immense with love, took them by the hand.
PSALM 106:45 MSG

You are loved—incredibly, sacrificially loved—by the King of kings. Doesn't that fill you with overwhelming joy? Can you sense His heart for you? God's love is not based on anything you have done or will ever do. No, that amazing love was poured out on Calvary and beckons us daily. You are loved—today and always!

Thank You, Father, for loving me with a deep, everlasting love. It is not a love I can fully comprehend, but I rest in it just the same.

Day 243

HOPE IN THE BLEAKEST CIRCUMSTANCE

*The LORD is good to those who hope
in him, to those who seek him.*
LAMENTATIONS 3:25 NCV

Hope is amazing. It can grow and thrive even in the bleakest circumstances. A prisoner of war suffers brutal abuse at the hands of his captors, but they cannot break his spirit or rob him of the hope that one day he will be free again. It's hope that keeps us moving forward, always looking for a better day. Hope is God's gift. Thank Him for it by placing your hope in Him. He is profoundly faithful.

*There is always hope in You, Lord. You are able to
do more than I can imagine in my wildest dreams.*

Day 244

GOD IS BY YOUR SIDE

Why, my soul, are you downcast? Why so disturbed
within me? Put your hope in God, for I will
yet praise him, my Savior and my God.
PSALM 42:5–6 NIV

People hope in many things—money, possessions, other people, power, fame, and status, even their own strength. None of those things have the power to sustain hope. But God does. Money and possessions can be gone in a moment, but He will never change. People will fail you, but He will never let you down. Power, fame, and status are remarkably fragile. Even your own strength will one day be gone. But God will still be by your side. Place your hope in Him.

I will praise You, my Father, no matter what.
Find me faithful all the days of my life, I pray.

Day 245

RADIATING JOY

For ye shall go out with joy, and be led forth with peace: the mountains and the hills shall break forth before you into singing, and all the trees of the field shall clap their hands.
ISAIAH 55:12 KJV

God reveals Himself in a million different ways, but perhaps the most breathtaking is through nature. The next time you're in a mountainous spot, pause and listen. Can you hear the sound of God's eternal song? Does joy radiate through your being? Aren't you filled with wonder and with peace? The Lord has, through the beauty of nature, given us a rare and glorious gift.

Creator God, You reveal Yourself in nature. Thank You for sunsets and rainbows, beaches and mountains. What beautiful gifts You give us!

Day 246

THE IMPORTANCE OF HOSPITALITY

*Do not forget to do good and to share with others,
for with such sacrifices God is pleased.*
HEBREWS 13:16 NIV

The true meaning of hospitality is opening up your heart to others, making them feel at home in your presence. That means you can be hospitable anywhere you are. Hospitality doesn't require a fancy house or a gourmet meal. When you reach out to someone else with love and acceptance, you have shown that person hospitality. Look around you. Ask God to show you people to whom you can minister just by opening your heart.

*God, show me how to be hospitable. Make me a faithful
steward of the resources You have given me.*

Day 247

WASHING AWAY OUR SORROWS

"Very truly I tell you, you will weep and mourn while the world rejoices. You will grieve, but your grief will turn to joy."
John 16:20 NIV

Imagine you're washing a load of white towels. One of them is badly stained. You add bleach to the wash load and let it run its cycle. Afterward, you can't tell which towel is which! The same is true when we allow God to wash away our sorrows. When all is said and done, all that remains is the joy!

You are bigger than my greatest sorrow, Lord. You bring beauty from ashes.

Day 248

THE CHILDREN
OF THE KING

Let the children of Zion be joyful in their King.
PSALM 149:2 NKJV

Hearing the voices of children lifted in joyous praise does something to the heart, doesn't it? Innocent, trusting, filled with pure happiness—their songs ring out for all to hear. Can you imagine how God must feel when we, His children, lift our voices, singing praise to Him? How it must warm His heart! What joy we bring our Daddy God when we praise!

Put a new song of praise on my lips, Lord. May I sing to You with wild abandon, and may my praise bring You glory and pleasure.

Day 249

HOSPITALITY TO STRANGERS

Do not neglect to show hospitality to strangers, for by doing this some have entertained angels without knowing it.
HEBREWS 13:2 NASB

It's easy enough to show hospitality to your family and friends, but God asks that you reach out to strangers as well. That takes courage. But God is pleased when you look past your own shyness and hesitation to touch the life of a person you don't know. Instead of focusing on how it makes you feel, think about how it could affect a stranger alone in a crowd. Your hospitality has the power to change a life for eternity.

*Your angels are watching over me all
day and all night, my Lord. Thank You!*

Day 250

UNTHINKABLE HUMILITY

With humility comes wisdom.
PROVERBS 11:2 NIV

The Bible says that Jesus is the only begotten Son of God, ruling and reigning with His Father from their heavenly throne room. And yet He did the unthinkable. He chose to be born as a baby, live as one of us, and then suffer reproach and abuse, finally death. He humbled Himself and allowed Himself to be placed on the cross—for you. His humility accomplished the plan of salvation. Imagine what your humble obedience to His will can accomplish.

Give me the humility of Christ, my Lord. May I humbly submit to His will and follow hard after Him.

Day 251

HUMILITY IS STRENGTH

By humility and the fear of the LORD
are riches, and honour, and life.
PROVERBS 22:4 KJV

If you think being humble will make you a doormat for others to walk on and take advantage of, you couldn't be more wrong. Many associate humility with weakness, but it is more closely defined as strength. It takes no special effort to behave proudly. Pride comes naturally to human beings. But humility—that's not so easy. It means making a choice to do the difficult thing, the God thing. Submit yourself to God and reap the benefits of humility.

God, replace any pride that You find in my
life with humility. In Jesus' name, amen.

Day 252

YOUR SECRET SINS

I know, my God, that you test the heart and are pleased with integrity. All these things I have given willingly and with honest intent.
1 CHRONICLES 29:17 NIV

Do you have a secret, something you are keeping hidden deep within, something that causes you to live in shame? You shouldn't think that you are keeping anything from God. He sees your heart. He knows all about you. And He wants to free you from the burden you are carrying. Confess your secret sins to Him—those you've committed and those committed against you. He will wash your heart clean. Then He will praise you as you live honestly and openly before Him.

God, clean every room of my heart. I want nothing more than to be open and transparent with You.

Day 253

ABIDING JOY

*Let Israel rejoice in him that made him: let
the children of Zion be joyful in their King.*
PSALM 149:2 KJV

Oh, the sound of children's joyful voices. It's like medicine for
the sick. Balm for the weary soul. God longs for His children
to rejoice in Him, to be joyful. And His desire for the family is
no less. What would be the point of living in a home where
everyone was sour and bitter? Today, ask the Lord to give
every member of your household a fresh dose of His abiding joy.

*Father, I pray for each one in my family to have a
special touch from You today. I ask that
we would walk in Your everlasting joy.*

Day 254

LIVING WITH INTEGRITY

Whoever walks in integrity walks securely.
PROVERBS 10:9 NIV

Choosing to do the right thing in a situation may be difficult, even painful. It could mean the loss of income, a broken relationship, or an embarrassing confrontation. But whatever it takes, keeping your integrity is vitally important. When you do what is right, you preserve your soul. You'll make mistakes—no doubt about that—but God is there to forgive you and help you stay on track in the future. When you choose integrity, you choose the Lord.

*God, give me the strength and desire to do
the right thing that I might honor You.*

Day 255

YOUR JOY TANK

"Until now you have not asked for anything in my name.
Ask and you will receive, and your joy will be complete."
JOHN 16:24 NIV

Have you ever faced a truly impossible situation—one so extreme that, unless God moved, everything else would surely crumble? God is a God of the impossible. And He wants us to ask, even when we're facing insurmountable obstacles. In fact, He wants us to know that only He can perform miracles. Our job? We're called to trust Him. Then, when those impossible situations turn around, our "joy tank" will be completely filled to overflowing!

God, I know You are able. I pray for Your
will above all else. You are a great God!

Day 256

GOD'S ULTIMATE LOVE

For God so loved the world, that he gave his only
begotten Son, that whosoever believeth in him
should not perish, but have everlasting life.
JOHN 3:16 KJV

The ultimate expression of love, one that will never be sur-passed, took place when God sent Jesus, His only Son, to die on the cross for our sins. "For God so loved. . .that He gave. . . ." That's what love does. It gives and gives and gives. Love is sacrifice—and in the person of Jesus Christ we witness the ultimate sacrifice. Today, as you ponder God's love for you, rejoice in the fact that He gave Himself willingly for you.

Lord, I memorized John 3:16 long ago. May it feel brand-new
to me today as I ponder Your great love for the world!

Day 257

LETTING GOD FIGHT YOUR BATTLES

Don't insist on getting even; that's not for you to do.
"I'll do the judging," says God. "I'll take care of it."
ROMANS 12:19 MSG

Many times when we are mistreated, we respond with vengeful thoughts and actions, forgetting that we look to a higher court—the authority of God. It isn't easy to lay down your offense, especially when your heart is aching for justice, but when you do, God is able to act on your behalf. Seeking revenge keeps you in a cycle of reciprocal hurt. Laying your grievance before God's high court frees you to move on. Trust God's pure justice and let Him fight your battles.

Lord, I leave all judgment up to You.
May I simply love others, no matter what.

Day 258

FOCUS ON THE BEAUTY

The Mighty One, God, the LORD, speaks and summons
the earth from the rising of the sun to where it sets.
From Zion, perfect in beauty, God shines forth.
PSALM 50:1–2 NIV

A child's face. A flowering pear tree. A rippling brook. A mountain's peak. All of these things overwhelm us with the magnitude of their beauty. Why? Because we can see that they were created by someone much larger than ourselves—someone incredibly creative and colorful. We are reminded of the awesomeness of God. Focus on the beauty He has placed in your world, and praise Him!

Creator God, You have made this world such a beautiful
place. Thank You for Your amazing creation.

Day 259

REMAINING PURE

The LORD loves the just and will not forsake his faithful ones.
PSALM 37:28 NIV

Often we cry for justice when we have been wronged, but not when we have wronged others. God wants us to care about both—because He does. Be sure that in all your transactions you require a high standard of fairness from yourself. Ask God to point out your blind spots so that your heart might remain pure before Him. When you mess up, be quick to make things right. God will be watching—and applauding.

God, may my heart be pure before You. Forgive me for the sins of yesterday, and keep me from sin today, I pray.

Day 260

THE SUFFERINGS
OF CHRIST

But rejoice inasmuch as you participate in the sufferings of Christ, so that you may be overjoyed when his glory is revealed.
1 PETER 4:13 NIV

Ever feel like you've signed on for the suffering but not the joy? We are called to be partakers in Christ's sufferings. We wouldn't really know Him if we didn't walk in the valleys occasionally. But, praise God, we are also partakers in His glorious resurrection. We have the power of the cross to spur us on! The time has come to trade in those sorrows. Reach for His unspeakable joy.

Lord, even in times of sorrow I will choose the joy available to me because of my relationship with You.

Day 261

KINDNESS TO THE UNDESERVING

*When the kindness and love of God our Savior appeared,
he saved us, not because of righteous things
we had done, but because of his mercy.*
TITUS 3:4–5 NIV

Do you find it easy to offer kindness to those you feel deserve it—but not to those who don't? That's a normal human response. But when you begin to understand the fullness of God's kindness to you personally, you're apt to see things in a different light. You weren't deserving or even grateful, and yet He was kind to you. He held nothing back. Being kind to those who don't deserve it is a powerful way to demonstrate your likeness to your heavenly Father.

*God, soften my heart toward those who are difficult to love.
May I demonstrate kindness to everyone around me.*

Day 262

LETTING GO

*Be kind to each other, tenderhearted,
forgiving one another, just as God
through Christ has forgiven you.*
EPHESIANS 4:32 NLT

Forgiveness is an interesting thing. When you release someone from the sin he or she has committed against you, it's almost like setting a bird free from a cage. You've freed that person to soar. And, in doing so, you've also freed yourself. No longer do you have to hold on to the bitterness or anger. Letting go means you can truly move forward with your life in joy!

*Free me, I pray, from the chains of unforgiveness.
Show me, Lord, those I need to forgive today. Amen.*

Day 263

BE KIND

Who can find a virtuous woman? for her price is far above rubies. . . . She openeth her mouth with wisdom; and in her tongue is the law of kindness.
PROVERBS 31:10, 26 KJV

Kindness is often misunderstood. It doesn't mean stepping back and letting others dictate to you. And it doesn't mean coddling and indulging others. It means being gentle, friendly, benevolent, and generous with another person, especially when there is no expectation of receiving anything from that person in return. You won't have to go looking for opportunities to be kind; they will appear on their own dozens of times a day. Be like your heavenly Father—be kind!

Lord, may I be a virtuous woman. I want others to know they can count on wisdom and kindness from me.

Day 264

THE BEAUTY OF SECOND CHANCES

*For his anger lasts only a moment, but his favor
lasts a lifetime; weeping may stay for the
night, but rejoicing comes in the morning.*

PSALM 30:5 NIV

Don't you love second chances? New beginnings? If only we could go back and redo some of our past mistakes—what better choices we'd make the second time around. Life in Jesus is all about the rebirth experience—the opportunity to start over. Each day is a new day, in fact. And praise God! The sorrows and trials of yesterday are behind us. With each new morning, joy dawns!

*Lord, thank You for all the chances You have given me.
Today is a new day, and I have a fresh start. I praise
You for the mercies and joys of each new day.*

Day 265

LEADING THROUGH SERVICE

"The greatest among you must become like the youngest, and the leader like one who serves."
LUKE 22:26 NRSV

Not everyone is called to be a leader, but if you feel God's call and sense you have been given the attributes you need to lead others, you are right to step out from the crowd and make it known. Just know that leadership in God's kingdom is a position of service. Like Moses and King David and the apostle Paul, God will humble you before He uses you. But if you're willing and obedient, He may use you to change the world.

God, use me as a leader, if it is Your will. Reveal the positions of service You have ordained for my life—day by day.

Day 266

A GOOD FOLLOWER

Be ye followers of me, even as I also am of Christ.
1 Corinthians 11:1 kjv

To be a good leader in God's kingdom, you must be a good follower—not of others, but of God. You aren't charged with setting the pace or cutting the path before you, but of keeping your eyes on the Lord and following His every move. That means you must know the principles He has laid out in the Bible and live in close and constant relationship with God. Leading others is a big responsibility and a great privilege.

*God, I will follow You all the days of my life. I will
not run ahead or lag behind. Help me to keep
in perfect step with You, my Father. Amen.*

Day 267

GOD SINGS OVER YOU

"The LORD your God is with you, the Mighty Warrior who saves. He will take great delight in you; in his love he will no longer rebuke you, but will rejoice over you with singing."
ZEPHANIAH 3:17 NIV

Picturing God celebrating over us is fun, isn't it? Can you imagine? He sings over us! He dances over us. He rejoices over us! What joy floods our souls as we realize our Father God, like a loving daddy, celebrates His love for His children. Today, reflect on the thought that God—with great joy in His voice—is singing over you.

Thank You, Lord, for such a deep, compassionate, unconditional love. You love me so much that You sing over me.

Day 268

FORGIVING OUR DEBTORS

"Forgive us our debts, as we also have forgiven our debtors."
MATTHEW 6:12 NIV

Is it true that God only forgives us to the extent that we forgive others? That's what His Word teaches! So it's important not to hold a grudge. It hurts you, and it hurts the one you're refusing to forgive. If you've been holding someone in unforgiveness, may today be the day when you let it go. Great joy comes both in forgiving and being forgiven.

God, today I choose to lay down the burden of unforgiveness. I choose to forgive _____ (fill in the blank with the name of someone you have struggled to forgive).

Day 269

STUDYING THE THINGS OF GOD

Let the wise listen and add to their learning.
PROVERBS 1:5 NIV

Being a Christian is all about being a student in the things of God. What a wonderful blessing! Each day you are charged with getting to know your heavenly Father better and becoming more like Him. That will sometimes be painful as you discard old thought patterns and behaviors in favor of new ones, but it will always be productive, transforming you into the person God created you to be. Stay close to Him, listen, and learn all you can.

Wise Father in heaven, fill me with wisdom that can come only from You. I ask this humbly in Your name. Amen.

Day 270

A FRESH START

When they saw the star, they rejoiced
with exceeding great joy.
MATTHEW 2:10 KJV

Can you imagine the wise men, gazing upon that star for the first time? Finally! The long-awaited day had come. What joy they must have felt in their hearts. Surely they could sense the beginning of a new era. The Gospel message is all about new beginnings. We rejoice every time we're given a chance to begin again. Praise God for the many times He has given you a fresh start.

God, I gaze into the night sky and imagine the star that
led the wise men to You. May I seek You and
worship You as Lord, just as the magi did.

Day 271

THE DEPTH OF HIS LOVE

Keep yourselves in the love of God, looking for the mercy of our Lord Jesus Christ unto eternal life.

JUDE 21 KJV

When you love the Lord and recognize His great love for you, being joyful is easy! Think of His marvelous deeds. Delight in His overwhelming love for His children. Recognize His daily blessings. Oh, may we never forget that the Lord our God longs for us to see the depth of His love for us—and to love Him fully in return.

No one can love me like You do, God. I only know in part now, but one day I will fully understand the depth of Your love.

Day 272

YOUR PROGRESS IN RIGHTEOUSNESS

Teach the righteous and they will gain in learning.
PROVERBS 9:9 NRSV

The number one characteristic of the unrighteous is their inability to learn. They make the same mistakes over and over, never recognizing their error or understanding that they have been given the power to change. You have seen the error of your ways and turned to God. Now continue to learn, continue to change, and continue to grow in the image of your heavenly Father. He is proud of your progress in righteousness.

Father, day by day I pray that I will learn more from Your Word that I can apply to my life. I want to walk in holiness.

Day 273

LIFTED FROM THE PIT

I waited patiently for the LORD. He turned to me and heard my cry. He lifted me out of the pit of destruction, out of the sticky mud. He stood me on a rock and made my feet steady.

PSALM 40:1–2 NCV

When you've been living in the pit, you can hardly imagine being lifted out of it. Oh, the joy of knowing that God can bring us out of even the deepest, darkest pit and place our feet on solid ground. Nothing is impossible with our Lord! If you're in a dark place today, call out to Him and watch as He delivers you. He will establish your steps. Praise Him!

God, thank You that You don't only comfort me while I'm in the pit. You come down into the pit. You follow me there and carry me out!

Day 274

LIVING TO
THE FULLEST

*The way you tell me to live is always right; help
me understand it so I can live to the fullest.*
PSALM 119:144 MSG

God has given us guidelines to live by—principles laid out in amazing detail in the Bible. Some say His rules are simply designed to bolster His ego. That's the same lie the devil told Eve when he tempted her to disobey God in the garden of Eden. "He's just trying to keep you from having something good," he taunted. Like any good parent, God has given us rules to ensure our safety and success. Living His way is always for your best.

*You came, Jesus, that I might have abundant
life. Help me to live life to the fullest!*

Day 275

SORROW INTO DANCING

You changed my sorrow into dancing. You took away
my clothes of sadness, and clothed me in happiness.
PSALM 30:11 NCV

Sometimes despair can feel like a deep well. You feel trapped. You can't seem to find your way out to the daylight above. Oh, friend! As deep as your well of sorrow might be, there is a deeper joy. Finding it requires resting your head against the Savior's chest, listening for His heartbeat until it beats in sync with yours. Today, dig deep and find that joy.

Jesus, hold me close. This sorrow is bigger than
I am, but it is no match for You, my Savior. Amen.

Day 276

LOOKING HEAVENWARD

"I have come that they may have life,
and have it to the full."
John 10:10 niv

A baby spends nine months in the mother's womb becoming the person God has created her or him to be. In comparison to this new person's life lived outside the womb, this preparation time is amazingly short. In the same way, our lives here on earth are relatively brief and intended as a time to grow and prepare for eternity with God. You are being groomed for eternal life. That will truly be living to the fullest measure.

May I always remember that the earth is not my home. I am but an alien here. Prepare my heart for my eternal home, Lord.

Day 277

YOU ARE SET FREE

Blessed is he whose transgression
is forgiven, whose sin is covered.
PSALM 32:1 NKJV

What if you were locked up in a prison cell for years on end? You waited for the day when the jailer would turn that key in the lock—releasing you once and for all. In a sense, experiencing God's forgiveness is like being set free from prison. Can you fathom the joy? Walking into the sunshine for the first time in years? Oh, praise Him for His forgiveness today!

You have replaced great darkness in my life with Your eternal light, Father. Thank You for saving my soul!

Day 278

FEELING LONELY

*I am convinced that. . .neither the present nor the future,
nor any powers, neither height nor depth, nor anything
else in all creation, will be able to separate us from
the love of God that is in Christ Jesus our Lord.*

ROMANS 8:38–39 NIV

You don't have to be alone to feel lonely. It's all about how you are connecting with those around you. Perhaps you are in a place in your life where you feel no one understands you and no one cares. This time in your life probably won't last long. You will make connections and the loneliness will pass, but until it does, remember that God has promised to always be there for you—to listen, to comfort, to encourage. He's as close as your prayer.

You tell me in Your Word, Father, to draw close to You and that You will draw close to me. Meet me here in my loneliness, I pray.

Day 279

SENDING YOUR LONELINESS PACKING

God sets the lonely in families, he leads
out the prisoners with singing.
Psalm 68:6 niv

Feeling alone or lonely is not God's will for you. He has gone to great lengths to include you in His family and surround you with spiritual brothers and sisters. Open your heart and let God help you make connections with His people. You will find that Christian fellowship goes deeper than any relationships you have had. It has permanence and variety. God wants to send your loneliness packing. Let Him set you squarely in His family.

Thank You, Lord, for putting Christian brothers and sisters in
my life. Allow me to connect on a deeper level with them.

Day 280

HIS UNCONDITIONAL LOVE

From everlasting to everlasting the LORD's love is with those who fear him, and his righteousness with their children's children.
PSALM 103:17 NIV

God loves you! It's not complicated or conditional—it's just a fact! Our human understanding can't comprehend the reason why, only that it's true. As much as you might want to explain it, dissect it, reason it out, you just can't. Instead of wrapping yourself in questions, wrap yourself in His love. Luxuriate in it just as you would a magnificent fur coat. God has spared no expense. He has given you the very best He has to offer.

I will bask in Your unfathomable love for me, Lord.
I will linger here awhile and meditate on the blessing
of being a daughter of the King of kings.

Day 281

LEARNING FROM MISTAKES

"All the earlier troubles, chaos, and pain are things of the past, to be forgotten. Look ahead with joy. Anticipate what I'm creating."
ISAIAH 65:17–18 MSG

We don't always get it right, do we? Sometimes we make mistakes. But our mistakes spur us on to begin again. We want to get it right the next time. And praise God! He gives us chance after chance, opportunity after opportunity. Let the joys of your past successes merge with the "spurs" of your past failings so that you can set out on a road of new beginnings.

Thank You for forgiving me, Lord. Your Word assures me that You cast it as far as the east is from the west.

Day 282

HIS RELENTLESS LOVE

"A new command I give you: Love one another. As I have loved you, so you must love one another. By this everyone will know that you are my disciples, if you love one another."
JOHN 13:34–35 NIV

God loves you relentlessly, completely, and in spite of your flaws and shortcomings. His greatest desire is for you to love in the same way. He asks you first of all to love Him in return and then to love others. When you love, you show that you are His child; you demonstrate who you are and what you're made of. That pleases your heavenly Father more than any great work you might do on His behalf. Live to please Him by loving others.

Father God, may my days be filled with seeking out ways to show love, and may I show love even in the face of adversity.

Day 283

CONSOLATION IN HIS LOVE

For we have great joy and consolation in thy love.
PHILEMON 7 KJV

Have you ever found yourself in need of consolation? Ever longed for someone to wrap his or her arms of love around you and make everything all right? God is that someone. We can take great consolation in His love, which is unchanging, everlasting, and abounding. Doesn't it bring joy to your heart to see how wide, how deep, and how long the Father's love is for His children?

God, when I fall into Your arms, I know that I am in a place where I am loved deeply and completely.

Day 284

HONORING MARRIAGE

Let marriage be held in honor by all.
Hebrews 13:4 nrsv

Since God placed the first man and woman in the garden of Eden, He has endorsed and blessed marriage. Except for those who have been set apart—like the apostle Paul—for singleness, God uses marriage as a tool to purify us. Through it He teaches lessons on faithfulness, trust, love, humility, service, gentleness, and much more. It is His refining fire. All the more reason to set your heart to live and grow within the boundaries of this holy union.

Teach me, Lord, to honor marriage as You desire it to be respected. I ask this in Jesus' name. Amen.

Day 285

LIVING SINGLE

"Your Maker is your husband—the LORD Almighty is his name."
ISAIAH 54:5 NIV

Women find themselves single all the time. Some are single by their own choice or as part of God's plan for their lives. Others may be divorced or widowed. If you are single for whatever reason, you may be surprised to learn that you are in a highly favored position. The Lord says that He is the One who will provide for you and defend you. You can look to Him for love and companionship. He is wiser and more faithful than any human husband.

God, You are all I need. In every season of my life, whether I am single or married, may I look to You first and foremost as my Husband. You are the Lord Almighty, who protects me and provides for me.

Day 286

GLORY IN
THE OUTDOORS

*God's glory is on tour in the skies, God-craft
on exhibit across the horizon.*

PSALM 19:1 MSG

Look outside right now; better yet, go outside. Daytime or nighttime, it doesn't matter. Just look around you. If you live in a concrete jungle, look up at the sky. Imagine for a moment the immensity of God's creation, the grandeur of it. And yet He calls mankind His most splendid creation—all the rest was called into being only to benefit His human creation. God values you above all else. Look up at the sky and consider that.

God, You are the Creator. I am but the created. I stand in awe of who You are and how much You love me. Amen.

Day 287

THIS IS THE DAY THAT THE LORD HAS MADE

This is the day that the LORD has made;
let us rejoice and be glad in it.
PSALM 118:24 NRSV

Are you having a hard day? Facing mounting problems? Maybe the bill collectors are calling or the kids are sick. You're at the end of your rope. Pause for a moment and remember: this is the day which the Lord has brought about. I will rejoice. It's His day and He longs for you to spend time with Him. Rejoice! It's the right choice.

Every single day is a gift, O God. I will rejoice,
even in the uncertainties of today. You have
my heart in the palm of Your hand.

Day 288

GOD'S ATTENTION TO DETAIL

"Walk out into the fields and look at the wildflowers."
MATTHEW 6:28 MSG

Our God cares about details. You see that care throughout His creation. Every species is unique and every creature is unique within its species. Human beings are created in His image and yet each is one of a kind. Flowers and trees are awash with color and refinement, even those growing along the highway, sown as it were by the wind. When you wonder if God is interested in the details of your life, consider the evidence demonstrated in nature. He is concerned about every aspect of your life—no matter how seemingly inconsequential.

You are not just a big-picture God. You are a God of the smallest details. Thank You for Your attention to my life.

Day 289

JOY DESPITE TEMPTATION

*Consider it pure joy, my brothers and sisters,
whenever you face trials of many kinds.*
JAMES 1:2 NIV

Temptations abound. We face them at every turn. On the television. In our conversations with friends. On the internet. Today, as you contemplate the many temptations that life has to offer, count it all joy! The enemy knows we belong to the King of kings. That's the only reason he places stumbling blocks in our way. Next time he rears his ugly head, joyfully use God's Word as a weapon to fight him off.

*God, give me the strength to say no to the things that
dishonor You. I want to choose a life of holiness.*

Day 290

RENEWING YOU

*And have put on the new self, which is being renewed
in knowledge in the image of its Creator.*
COLOSSIANS 3:10 NIV

Is there someone in your life whom you've been praying for, for years? Maybe sometimes you're tempted to believe he or she will never come to the Lord. Today, ponder the new beginnings in your own life. Hasn't God recreated you? Renewed you? Won't He do the same for others? Feel the joy rise up as you ponder the possibilities. Pray for that friend or loved one to "put on the new self."

*God, I believe that You are powerful enough to save _____
(fill in the name of someone you are praying for).
Work in his/her life, I ask in Jesus' name.*

Day 291

ENTERING HIS SPLENDOR

*Splendor and majesty are before him; strength
and joy are in his dwelling place.*
1 CHRONICLES 16:27 NIV

In Old Testament days, only the high priest could enter the Holy of Holies to spend intimate time with God. However, when Jesus died on the cross, the veil in the temple was torn in two. We now have free access to the Holy of Holies, and Jesus bids us to enter—often! He longs to spend time with us in that place. And oh, what joy, when we enter in! Make that choice today.

*Thank You, God, that I may come into Your presence.
Because of Christ, I have free access to my Father.*

Day 292

THE IMPORTANCE
OF PATIENCE

Patience is better than strength.
PROVERBS 16:32 NCV

Our electronic world does not encourage patience. Internet providers tout newer, faster technologies. What used to take days, even weeks, can now be done in minutes. Not everything can be rushed though. God still does things in His own way and in His own timing. He won't be bullied or hurried. He wants to strengthen and test your faith. When you feel impatient while waiting for God to move on your behalf, resolve to trust Him. Surrender yourself to Him. You can be sure that He knows best.

*I surrender my impatience to You, Father. Help me as
I wait. You know what is best for my life. I trust You.*

Day 293

SPIRITUAL GUARDRAILS

Stay alert! Watch out for your great enemy, the devil. He prowls around like a roaring lion, looking for someone to devour.

1 Peter 5:8 nlt

Dear God, help me to erect proper boundaries in my life. I don't want to fall prey to a sin simply because I'm not being careful. Just like guardrails on a dangerous mountain highway, boundaries in my life keep me closer to center and farther away from the cliffs. I know Satan is plotting my destruction, but Your power is greater. Let me cooperate with Your grace by a careful lifestyle and a discerning spirit. In Christ's name, amen.

In the name of Jesus, I ask that Satan be cast far away from my life. I want nothing to do with his traps and tricks.

Day 294

JUST WAIT

*Be still before the L*ORD *and wait patiently for him.*
PSALM 37:7 NIV

Do you remember as a child waiting for Christmas morning or for the time to open your presents on your birthday? "Just wait. It will all happen in due time," your mother would say. God won't withhold from you just to be cruel or to make a point, but He does see the big picture, and He knows the right when, where, and how. So don't get anxious, just wait. You will see what God has promised you—all in due time.

I am so rarely still, God. Calm my heart in
these moments, I pray. I will wait for You.

Day 295

OPEN YOUR HEART

*You, LORD, give true peace to those who
depend on you, because they trust you.*
ISAIAH 26:3 NCV

Peace is to the kingdom of God what oxygen is to the atmosphere. Considering this truth, you may be wondering why you so often feel agitated and anxious. Think of it this way: though oxygen permeates the air around us, we must breathe it into our lungs for it to do us any good. You must choose to let God rule in your heart. You must invite Him in. As you open your heart to Him, peace will follow.

*Peace can be found in nothing or no one but You, Lord.
I breathe in Your peace as I face this day. Amen.*

Day 296

MOVE TOWARD PEACE

Let the peace of Christ rule in your hearts, since as
members of one body you were called to peace.
Colossians 3:15 niv

God often uses peace as a way of giving His children guidance. When you are praying about an important decision or life choice, you should pay close attention to the amount of peace you have concerning it. In any case, you should not move when your peace is replaced by a sense of anxiety or unrest. Move back in the other direction until peace comes. You will never go wrong as long as you follow the peace.

May Your peace be my compass through life, heavenly
Father. I will walk on the paths You have laid out for me.

Day 297

POWER TO THE WEAK

*[God] gives strength to the weary and
increases the power of the weak.*
ISAIAH 40:29 NIV

When Jesus walked the earth, widows and orphans were the most disadvantaged members of society. They were essentially powerless in a culture where women were not valued except through their husbands. These disenfranchised women are often mentioned in the New Testament; however, Jesus made it clear that they were to be treated kindly, with respect, and to be cared for. He raised them from their less-than-nothing status to full acceptance in the body of believers. You are never powerless when you belong to Him.

*On my weakest day, I have great strength because my power
source is not found in myself but in You, my eternal God.*

Day 298

A WOMAN'S WORK

[Be] strengthened with all power according to his glorious might so that you may have great endurance and patience.
COLOSSIANS 1:11 NIV

There aren't enough hours in the day to do a woman's work. No wonder we often feel exhausted and unhappy. The Bible says that there is a remedy for our endless activity. He strengthens us, empowering us to push through and get our jobs done. Sometimes He does that by empowering us to say no when we should, rest when we should, and keep our lives balanced. Ask Him for a power transfusion for your life.

Moment by moment, Lord, I ask You for the endurance and patience I need to carry out the duties set before me. Amen.

Day 299

ENSNARED BY
THE ENEMY

*And lead us not into temptation, but deliver us
from evil: For thine is the kingdom, and
the power, and the glory, for ever. Amen.*
Matthew 6:13 kjv

Have you ever been ensnared by the enemy? Led into temptation?
Caught in his trap? When you give your heart to Christ, you are
set free from your past, delivered from the bondage of sin. Talk
about a reason to celebrate! Nothing is more glorious than being
led out of a prison cell into the sunlight. Oh, joyous freedom!
Today, praise God for the things He has delivered you from.

*Nothing is beyond Your deliverance, Lord. I have
been set free from the chains of my past!*

Day 300

BROUGHT FORTH WITH JOY

He brought forth his people with
joy, and his chosen with gladness.
PSALM 105:43 KJV

Have you ever been delivered out of a terrible situation? Lifted out of it, unharmed? Were you stunned when it happened? Had you given up? God is in the deliverance business! And when He lifts us out of impossible situations, we are overwhelmed with joy and we're surprised! Why do we doubt His goodness? The next time you're in a tough spot, expect to be "brought forth with joy."

Come, Lord Jesus, into this valley with me.
Set my feet on the mountaintop again, I pray.

Day 301

A CHOSEN PEOPLE

*Ye are a chosen generation, a royal priesthood,
an holy nation, a peculiar people; that ye should
shew forth the praises of [God] who hath called
you out of darkness into his marvellous light.*

1 PETER 2:9 KJV

Your life is a song of praise that rises to God your Father. He revels in your decision to take His hand and step out of darkness into light. It's what He has worked so hard to accomplish. It's why He sent His Son, Jesus, to live and die and rise again. You are His trophy, His prize, the sure and certain reward of His great sacrifice. Each time you say yes to life, yes to love, yes to eternal values, you are praising Him.

*Thank You for calling me out of darkness
and into glorious light, Lord Jesus. Amen.*

Day 302

WORSHIP WITH ABANDON

Let us come before His presence with thanksgiving;
let us shout joyfully to Him with psalms.
PSALM 95:2 NKJV

Sometimes we forget that the Lord loves us to praise joyfully. We get caught up in tradition or maybe we just feel uncomfortable worshipping with abandon. The Lord loves a happy heart—and He truly enjoys it when we make a joyful noise, lifting up our praises (our psalms) for all to hear. So break out of the box today! Be set free to worship!

I will sing to You songs of praise and thanksgiving.
I will make a joyful noise unto You, Lord.

Day 303

BEING USED BY GOD

Become the kind of container God can use to present any and every kind of gift to his guests for their blessing.
2 Timothy 2:21 msg

Want to reach the end of your life feeling completely fulfilled? Want to know true joy? Then allow the Lord to use you. Does that idea contradict what you've been taught in this "me first" society? Being "used" by God is far different from being "used" by people. Being usable is our goal, our ambition. Today, offer your gifts and abilities to the Lord so that they can be used for His purpose.

Use me, Lord. Use all of me for Your glory. Use my gifts and talents, my resources and my time. They all belong to You.

Day 304

YOUR LIFE OF PRAISE

I will praise You, O Lord, with my whole heart. . . .
I will sing praise to Your name, O Most High.
PSALM 9:1–2 NKJV

Your life is a form of praise, but your words of praise are even more precious to your heavenly Father. His Holy Spirit who lives within you carries them straight to His throne. Why are your praises so dear to Him? Because, unlike His other creatures, your praises are not innate. They are the free expression of your heart. You chose Him when you could have chosen so many others. Lift your voice to Him. It brings Him great joy.

O God Most High, I lift You up and praise Your name. You are above and before and beyond all things. You are the God of my soul, and I will never stop praising You.

Day 305

PRAYERFUL THANKS

Pray and ask God for everything you need, always giving thanks.
Philippians 4:6 ncv

Prayer is quite simply conversation with God. What a joyous privilege we have to be able to speak to Him—almighty God—whenever we desire. How could you ever get enough of those times with Him? Meet with Him often to talk about your life. Tell Him your troubles and leave your worries at His feet. Confess your sins to Him and receive His forgiveness. Tell Him how much you love Him and how grateful you are to be His daughter. He's always ready to listen.

In this moment, I come before You with a thankful heart. I am thankful for _____ (tell God what you are thankful for). In Jesus' name, amen.

Day 306

KEEP SEEKING HIM

*"When you call upon me and come and pray to me,
I will hear you. When you search for me, you will
find me; if you seek me with all your heart."*
JEREMIAH 29:12–13 NRSV

Is there a great need in your life? Something you have struggled with and can't seem to find the answer for? God says to bring it to Him—not just once but again and again. Keep asking. Keep reminding Him of His promises. Like a child who campaigns for a new bike, never give up. Seek God and keep on seeking Him. He hears you every time, and He will reward your persistence and your patience after He proves your heart.

I seek You earnestly and persistently, Lord, with all my heart. I know You want all of me, not just part. Amen.

Day 307

FACING IMPOSSIBLE ODDS

"This day is holy to our Lord. Do not grieve,
for the joy of the LORD is your strength."
NEHEMIAH 8:10 NIV

Is it possible to have joy in the middle of catastrophic circumstances? What if you're facing the loss of a job? A devastating illness? The death of a loved one? Can you really look beyond your grief to find the joy? Our very strength comes from the joy God places inside us, and we need that strength even more when we're facing seemingly impossible odds! Today, may God's joy strengthen you from the inside out.

Even in my disappointment, Lord, I will dig deep and draw
upon the joy that You have planted in my spirit. Amen.

Day 308

THE PRESENCE OF GOD

Blessed are those who have learned to acclaim you,
who walk in the light of your presence, LORD.
PSALM 89:15 NIV

Close your eyes and imagine yourself sitting on the beach, a warm breeze tickling your skin and the comforting sound of waves breaking on the shore. Or think of yourself in a garden, enchanting fragrances and the sounds of songbirds all around you. Place yourself anywhere, but know that nothing can compare to being in God's presence. The treasures of the universe are stored there, His love surrounds you, and peace flows like a beautiful river. Come and enjoy.

I will walk in the light of Your presence,
Lord. You alone are enough for me.

Day 309

GIVE THEM SOMETHING TO TALK ABOUT

Everyone has heard about your obedience, so I rejoice because of you; but I want you to be wise about what is good, and innocent about what is evil.

ROMANS 16:19 NIV

Ever been caught in a situation where people were talking about you behind your back? Maybe folks you loved and trusted? How did that make you feel? Well, how would you feel if you found out people were talking about you because of your obedience? Wow! That's a different thing altogether. Let them talk! May our joyful obedience to the Lord win us a spot in many cheerful conversations!

Lord, may I be wise about what is good and innocent about what is evil. In Jesus' name, amen.

Day 310

CORPORATE WORSHIP

"Where two or three gather in my name, there am I with them."
MATTHEW 18:20 NIV

God loves to be where His people are. His Holy Spirit dwells in each one of them, but when believers come near each other, something heavenly happens—not only does He dwell in them, but He also fills the distance between them. In this atmosphere, the impossible becomes possible and love becomes manifest. God urges you to meet together with other believers regularly. He knows what can happen when you do.

As I pray with others, Lord, You remind me that You are there with us. You, the God of the entire universe, hear our prayers.

Day 311
BE ON YOUR GUARD

*"Watch and pray, lest you enter into temptation.
The spirit indeed is willing, but the flesh is weak."*
MARK 14:38 NKJV

We have to be on our guard for unexpected attacks. Temptation can strike at any point. We might feel strong—might convince ourselves we're not vulnerable—but our flesh is weak! We often end up giving in, even when we're determined not to. Today, ask the Lord to prepare you for any temptations that might come your way. Then, with joy in your heart, be on your guard!

Protect me from temptation, I pray, Lord. Keep me strong. Amen.

Day 312

YOUR FIRST PRIORITY

Fear God and keep his commandments,
for this is the duty of all mankind.
ECCLESIASTES 12:13 NIV

God knows how busy your life is. But as you move from task to task throughout your day, remember to stay connected to Him. Keep the conversation going between the two of you, and His love, joy, and peace will flow to you all day long. God should be your first priority because it is through His wisdom and strength that you accomplish your other priorities.

Above all else, Lord—that is where You desire to be in my life. I want to keep You my number one priority. Amen.

Day 313

ETERNAL PRIORITIES

*Seek those things which are above, where Christ is,
sitting at the right hand of God. Set your mind
on things above, not on things on the earth.*
COLOSSIANS 3:1–2 NKJV

Human beings can be hopelessly shortsighted. But the person who sees past today and plans for eternity has both the present and the future in mind. When you accepted Christ's sacrifice for you on the cross and asked God to forgive your sins, your future in heaven was sealed. But the Bible also talks about laying up treasure in heaven. Place your priorities on those things that are eternal rather than on those things that are just for this world alone.

*I will focus on the things that are greater than this
world. I will dwell on You and Your ways, Lord.*

Day 314

FOCUS ON HIM, NOT YOUR FEARS

The LORD your God will lead you and protect you on every side.
ISAIAH 52:12 GNT

We all have fears—fear of harm, fear of losing a child, fear of being alone, and fear of failure. When your fears rise up and threaten to overcome you, when you feel sick in the pit of your stomach and your heart aches with anxiety, remember this— God is with you, every day, every hour, every moment. Focus on Him, really focus, and you will see that your fears are nothing more than speculation that is swept away in His presence.

God, my fears look small when I gaze into Your glorious face. You are big enough to handle anything I am afraid of. Amen.

Day 315

MAKING DISCIPLES

"Go therefore and make disciples of all the nations."
MATTHEW 28:19 NKJV

Have you ever pondered the mandate in Matthew's Gospel to go into the entire world and preach the Gospel? Ever feel like you're not doing your part? God calls us to be witnesses where we are—to bloom where we're planted. Imagine the joy of leading a neighbor or a friend to the Lord. Instead of fretting over not doing enough, delight in the fact that you are usable right where you are.

Help me to be a witness right where I am,
Lord. Make me bold, I pray. Amen.

Day 316

THE PATH OF LIFE

You make known to me the path of life; in your presence there is fullness of joy; at your right hand are pleasures forevermore.
PSALM 16:11 ESV

When we stay on God's path—His road—we experience fullness in every area. And if we stick close to Him, which we are called to do, we will experience joy—not just now, in this life, but forevermore. Can you imagine a joy that never ends? Draw near to the Lord. In His presence you will find fullness of joy.

I love to spend time with You, Father.
In Your presence is where I find pure joy!

Day 317

YOUR HEAVENLY FATHER'S CONSTANT CARE

The LORD watches over all who love him.
PSALM 145:20 NIV

Like any loving parent, your heavenly Father keeps you in His constant care, never letting you out of His sight. You have no reason to fear, for He is always with you, ready to face whatever comes your way. He will not fail you. In some cases, He will warn you ahead of time. In others, He will supernaturally remove you from a dangerous situation. And sometimes He will hold your hand as you walk through fire. He is your God!

Whether You calm the storm or lead me through it, I will trust in You, Lord. Amen.

Day 318

THE COST OF DISOBEDIENCE

If they obey and serve him, they shall spend their days in prosperity, and their years in pleasures.
Job 36:11 KJV

If you knew that your disobedience was going to cost you dearly, would you be more inclined to obey? If you knew that your obedience would be rewarded, would that spur you on to do the right thing? God's Word convinces us that our days can be spent in prosperity and our years in pleasures if we will simply obey and serve the Lord. Oh, the joy of obedience!

Keep me from disobedience, Father. I want to walk in obedience that I might please You and be blessed.

Day 319

HIS PROMISE OF CARE

God will generously provide all you need. Then you
will always have everything you need and
plenty left over to share with others.
2 Corinthians 9:8 NLT

God has promised to take care of you, but it doesn't stop there. He wants to provide for you abundantly—so much that you can share it with others. His provision isn't limited to money. He is the provider of all you need. If you need joy, He'll give it to you with enough to share. If you need wisdom, it's there for you as well. Whatever you have on your list—ask Him for it. Then trust Him.

You are my provider, Lord. Just as You provided
manna for the Israelites in the wilderness,
You will meet each of my needs in due time.

Day 320

JOY IS A CHOICE

*But rejoice, inasmuch as ye are partakers of Christ's
sufferings; that, when his glory shall be revealed,
ye may be glad also with exceeding joy.*
1 PETER 4:13 KJV

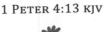

We want to know Christ—both in the glory of His resurrection
and in the fellowship of His sufferings. If we're open to knowing Him in both ways, then we have to be vulnerable. Finding
a balance is key. It really is possible to go through times of
suffering and still maintain your joy. After all, joy is a choice.

*Even if it means I will suffer, I will follow You, Lord.
Help me to rejoice even during times of suffering.*

Day 321

HIS PERFECT TIMING

"Your Father knows what you need before you ask him."
MATTHEW 6:8 NIV

God wants you to have everything you need for a great life. But sometimes we pray and things don't happen when we expect them to. You must trust that His timing is perfect. None of us live in a vacuum. Sometimes your request requires compliance on the part of other people, and they may not be prompt to respond. Don't give up. God will answer your prayer in the perfect way at the perfect time.

God, I come to You earnestly, asking that You hear this prayer. (State the prayers of your heart here.) I know You hear my requests and will do what is best for me.

Day 322

PERSEVERING UNDER TRIAL

Blessed is the one who perseveres under trial because, having stood the test, that person will receive the crown of life that the Lord has promised to those who love him.

JAMES 1:12 NIV

We are so focused on the joys of this life that we sometimes forget the exquisite joys yet to come in the next. Enduring and overcoming temptation can bring us great satisfaction here on earth, but imagine the crown of life we're one day going to receive. Nothing can compare! Oh, the joy of eternal life. Oh, the thrill of that joyous crown.

Even in the midst of trials, I will stand with You. You are my reward.

Day 323

BROTHERLY LOVE

*Be devoted to one another in love. Honor
one another above yourselves.*
ROMANS 12:10 NIV

Jesus' ultimate sacrifice—laying down His life so that all humanity could experience eternal life—showed true devotion. His willingness to go to the cross gave you the opportunity to experience an intimacy with God that was not available before. Likewise, you can honor others with the same love. That strength and power of love resides within you. God gave you the ability to show His love to everyone you meet. Be bold! Be courageous! Love like Jesus does! It's in you!

*God, help me to put others above myself. That is sometimes
hard to do. I want to love like Jesus loves. Amen.*

Day 324

OBEDIENCE BRINGS JOY

I know also, my God, that You test the heart
and have pleasure in uprightness.
1 Chronicles 29:17 nkjv

Everyone wants to be happy, right? We know that our obedience to the Lord results in a life of great joy. But our obedience does something else too. It brings pleasure to our heavenly Father. When we live uprightly, God is pleased. Today, instead of focusing on your own happiness, give some thought to putting a smile on His face.

May my life be pleasing to You, Lord.
I want to put a smile on Your face today.

Day 325

THE POWER OF FAMILY

Kinsfolk are born to share adversity.
PROVERBS 17:17 NRSV

Your family holds a powerful place in your life. The same is true of your sisters and brothers in the Lord. They know your greatest strengths and most intimate weaknesses—but with a different agenda. The family of God is to build you up in the area of your weakness and draw from you in the area of your strength. Though often painful, this is a process designed to make you strong and fruitful. There is great reward in enduring the adversity of relationships.

Lord, may I learn a little bit more about myself
from my Christian community. May I grow
in the process and be open to refinement.

Day 326

WALKING UPRIGHT

Folly is joy to him who is destitute of discernment,
but a man of understanding walks uprightly.
PROVERBS 15:21 NKJV

Ever noticed that people who have something to hide don't look others in the eye? Their gaze shifts up, down, and all around. But those who walk uprightly can look others in the eye without guilt or shame. Live wisely. Hold your head high. Look folks in the eye. Let wisdom lead the way and watch as joy follows!

I find my confidence in You alone, Lord. Help me to walk
uprightly and to follow in Your wise ways each day. Amen.

Day 327

INEXPLICABLE JOY

Let the peace of Christ rule in your hearts, since as members of one body you were called to peace. And be thankful.
COLOSSIANS 3:15 NIV

Have you ever unexpectedly received really great news? Remember the inexplicable joy that rose up as you received it? You didn't conjure it up; the joy came quite naturally. Today the news is good! God loves you! He cares for your needs and surrounds you on every side. He is your defense. As you contemplate these things, watch out! Joy is sure to fill your heart!

What Good News! Jesus loves me, this I know, for the Bible tells me so. I will rejoice in the Good News of the Gospel!

Day 328

SHAPING THE PERFECT YOU

Create in me a pure heart, O God,
and renew a steadfast spirit within me.
PSALM 51:10 NIV

No two snowflakes are alike. No two sunsets are ever exactly the same. Your Creator delivers a masterpiece with every stroke of artistry He inspires. You are no different. With each touch of His hand, with every letter you read in His Word, He changes your heart from old to new—forming you into His image. You become more like Him each moment you spend with Him. Your Creator makes all things new—and He's continually shaping the perfect you!

Father God, You are recreating me daily, Lord, to look a little
more like You. Thank You for renewing my spirit. Amen.

Day 329

COMPLETE JOY

*"I have told you this so that my joy may be
in you and that your joy may be complete."*
JOHN 15:11 NIV

Do you realize that joy is limitless? It knows no boundaries.
Jesus poured Himself out on that cross at Calvary—giving
everything—so that you could experience fullness of joy. Even
now, God longs to make Himself known to you in a new and
unique way. May you burst at the seams with this limitless joy
as you enter His presence today.

*Thank You for complete joy, Lord. Help me
to overflow with the fullness of Your joy.*

Day 330

CULTIVATING YOUR RELATIONSHIP

Though outwardly we are wasting away,
yet inwardly we are being renewed day by day.
2 CORINTHIANS 4:16 NIV

Your relationship with God is alive. It's living and breathing and requires nourishment to survive. Much like tributaries pour into lakes and rivers, you give out of your spirit into all you do. When you give out, you can drain your reserves. God wants you full. Fill up as you renew your spirit and mind daily with His Word and in His presence. You're a life-giving river of living water. Fill up, pour out, and fill up again!

Renew me day by day as I seek You
through Your Word and prayer, Lord.

Day 331

REFRESHING YOUR SOUL

"Repent, then, and turn to God, so that your sins may be wiped out, that times of refreshing may come from the Lord."
ACTS 3:19 NIV

Think of a chalkboard, like the one your teacher used in school. What if every bad thing you'd ever done was written on the board? Now envision the teacher taking the eraser and blotting it all out. Wiping it away. As you watch those sins disappear, you are flooded with joy. Your soul is refreshed. The past no longer holds you back. Give your heart to the Lord, and watch the refreshing come!

*I lay down the past and run with wild abandon
into my future—free, forgiven, cleansed
by the blood of Christ, my Lord. Amen.*

Day 332

RESPECTING GOD'S WORK

A kindhearted woman gains honor.
PROVERBS 11:16 NIV

As you grow in God, you begin to demonstrate His character and nature in your thoughts, attitudes, and behavior. Through you, His goodness becomes evident to others, and their respect for you increases. This will happen not because you demand it but because it is a natural response to God's glory. For the same reason, you must respect yourself—casting down thoughts of inferiority and unworthiness. Respect God's presence and work within you.

Lord, I accept and respect Your presence in my life.
I can feel You at work within me, and I give You thanks.

Day 333

DEEP ROOTS

"Those on the rocky ground are the ones who receive the word with joy when they hear it, but they have no root. They believe for a while, but in the time of testing they fall away."
LUKE 8:13 NIV

Imagine a sturdy oak tree, one that's been growing for decades. Its roots run deep. It is grounded. When the storms of life strike, that tree is going to stand strong. Now think of your own roots. Do they run deep? When temptations strike, will you stand strong? Dig into God's Word. Receive it with joy. Let it be your foundation. Plant yourself and let your roots run deep.

God, Your Word is the rock on which I stand. Amen.

Day 334

LET IT FLOW

And these things write we unto you, that your joy may be full.
1 John 1:4 kjv

Imagine you're in the process of filling a glass with water and accidentally pour too much in. The excess goes running down the sides, splashing your hand and anything else it comes in contact with. That's how it is when you're overflowing with joy from the inside out. You can't help but spill out onto others, and before long, they're touched too. So let it flow!

May I overflow with joy that comes only from You,
my Father in heaven. I am abundantly blessed. Amen.

Day 335

SAY HIS NAME

Knowledge begins with respect for the LORD.
PROVERBS 1:7 NCV

The Hebrews who walked across the Red Sea had such a reverence for God that they never said His name out loud. They had great respect for Him. Though your relationship with God is much different today, He still desires your respect. You are His child and He adores you. You are privileged to show Him your admiration. Give Him respect through praise, worship, and adoration. He wants to hear you—His precious child—say His name!

Lord, I admire You. I respect You. I praise You, for Your name is great. I worship You, for You are above all others. You are the one true God. Amen.

Day 336

CONSIDER THE LILIES

Consider the lilies how they grow: they toil not, they spin not.
LUKE 12:27 KJV

Sometimes we look at our job as our provision. We say things like, "I work for my money." While it's true that we work hard (and are rewarded with a paycheck), we can't forget that God is our provider. If He cares for the lilies of the field—flowers that bloom for such a short season—then how much more does He care for us, His children? What joy—realizing that God loves us enough to provide for our needs.

God, You are Jehovah Jireh. You are the Lord who provides. I will rest in Your provision for my life. Amen.

Day 337

GOD'S PROVISION

Everything God created is good, and to be received with thanks.
1 Timothy 4:4 msg

Sometimes we walk through seasons of blessing and forget to be grateful. It's easy, with the busyness of life, to overlook the fact that Someone has made provision to cover the monthly bills. Someone has graced us with good health. Someone has given us friends and loved ones to share our joys and sorrows. Today, pause a moment and thank the Lord for the many gifts He has poured out. Hem in those blessings!

God, help me to count my blessings and name them one by one. Everything I have comes from Your hand.

Day 338

PRIVATE TIME WITH GOD

Surely the righteous will praise your name,
and the upright will live in your presence.
PSALM 140:13 NIV

Have you ever gone camping in a tent? What if you had a special place—a quiet, private place like that tent—where you could dwell with God? A private place of worship? Wouldn't you want to linger inside that holy habitat, separating yourself from the outside world? Pitch your tent today and spend some time inside with the King of kings.

Lord, I linger here in Your presence. I have found a quiet moment, and I will be still and know that You are God. Amen.

Day 339

THE IMPORTANCE
OF HARD WORK

*Whatever you do, work at it with all your heart, as
working for the Lord, not for human masters, since
you know that you will receive an inheritance from the
Lord as a reward. It is the Lord Christ you are serving.*
Colossians 3:23–24 niv

Sometimes it may feel like your hard work goes unnoticed. Maybe you're tempted to slack off like the other guy, telling yourself that no one will ever know. God knows your heart. The One who holds the future in His hands sees your faithfulness. He has entrusted you with much responsibility because He knows He can count on you. He will reward you and will bring you into a place of blessing. Expect it and believe He'll do it. God applauds you!

*Father, to whom much is given, much is required. Find me
faithful in my work and in all my responsibilities, I pray. Amen.*

Day 340

YOUR AWESOME CREATOR

The heavens declare the glory of God;
the skies proclaim the work of his hands.
PSALM 19:1 NIV

Oh, the wonder of God's creation! Who could paint the skies such a brilliant blue? And who could give such detail to a tiny blade of grass? Only our creative Lord! Spend some time outdoors with Him today, soaking in the beauty of your surroundings. Allow the joy to permeate your soul, and give thanks to our awesome God, Creator of all.

God of heaven and earth, You are an artistic Creator.
Thank You for the beauty of Your world. Amen.

Day 341

THE WEIGHT OF RESPONSIBILITY

There are different kinds of service, but the same Lord.
1 CORINTHIANS 12:5 NIV

You may feel the weight of responsibilities you have been given. God made your shoulders broad enough to carry all that has been assigned to you. Embrace your responsibility, knowing that God has given you grace to carry it—and that when it seems too heavy, He's there to help you. He won't leave you alone to do what He has asked you to do. He won't let you fall under the weight. He won't condemn you for stumbling under the load. He's there for you!

Almighty God, grant me a portion of Your strength,
that together we might shoulder the weight of all the
responsibilities You have entrusted me with in this life.

Day 342

A HEAVENLY CHORUS

*Sing, O heavens; and be joyful, O earth; and break forth into
singing, O mountains: for the LORD hath comforted
his people, and will have mercy upon his afflicted.*
ISAIAH 49:13 KJV

Imagine you're walking through a meadow on a dewy morning. The sweet smell of dawn lingers in the air. Suddenly, like
a skilled orchestra, the heavens above begin to pour out an
unexpected song of joy. You close your eyes, overwhelmed by
the majesty of the moment. God's Word tells us the heavens
and the earth are joyful, so tune in to their chorus today.

*You are known, Lord, through Your majestic
creation. All of creation will sing Your praise.*

Day 343

A SPIRITUAL POWER NAP

The beloved of the LORD rests in safety—the High God surrounds him all day long—the beloved rests between his shoulders.
DEUTERONOMY 33:12 NRSV

When you think of rest, you probably think of a nap or picture yourself soaking in a tub. While you need physical rest, God wants your soul well rested and full of His presence too. Read encouraging Bible passages that build your faith. Spend time with Him in prayer. You'll feel like you've had a spiritual power nap. You'll come away rested and strengthened in your soul, safe from the assaults of the day.

I find my rest in You, God. You are my hiding place and my refuge, a very present help in times of trouble. Amen.

Day 344

CHILDLIKE JOY

I will greatly rejoice in the LORD,
my soul shall be joyful in my God.
ISAIAH 61:10 NKJV

As children we used to sing, "I've got the joy, joy, joy, joy down in my heart!" We bounced up and down in our seats with great glee. Do you still have that joy? Has it lingered into your adulthood? Do you sense it to the point where you could come bounding from your chair, ready to share what He has given you with a lost and dying world? Oh, for such a childlike joy!

Lord, even though not every moment is filled
with happiness, I claim Your joy daily. Amen.

Day 345

SINGING OFF-KEY

*O come, let us sing unto the Lord: let us make
a joyful noise to the rock of our salvation.*
Psalm 95:1 kjv

Do you love to sing praises to God? Perhaps your voice isn't the best. Maybe you can't carry a tune in a bucket, but you long to praise God anyway. Go ahead and do it! We're told in God's Word to "make a joyful noise" to the Lord. We're not told it has to be with a trained voice. So lift up those praises! He accepts them, on key or off!

*God, hear my heart when I sing Your praises. Please
accept my praise offering. In Jesus' name, amen.*

Day 346

EVEN GOD RESTED

On the seventh day God. . .rested from all his work.
GENESIS 2:2 NIV

Many women put in forty hours a week at a full-time job and then come home to care for the house and family. Don't forget to take time out for you. If God rested after working all week, then it's important to take care of yourself. The list of things to do will wait. Press the pause button and rest your mind, body, and emotions. You're precious and valuable to God and all of those who love you. You're worth it. Take a moment and relax.

*I will rest in the Lord my God. I will set aside time
to be still and know that You are God. Please
refresh my spirit as I rest in You, Lord.*

Day 347

REWARDING KINDNESS

*You know that the Lord will reward
each one for whatever good they do.*
EPHESIANS 6:8 NIV

Have you ever received a reward for an act of kindness? Maybe you returned a wallet or found a lost pet. So often the goodness of God goes unnoticed. He gives with open hands, never expecting anything in return, because His motivation is love. He loved you enough to give up everything. You can give something to God. Become the rewarder! Let Him know that His grace and mercy have not gone unnoticed. Reward Him with your praise and thanksgiving.

*Thank You for Your grace and mercy in my life, God.
I recognize the great gift of Your unmerited favor.*

Day 348

THE GIFT OF RELATIONSHIPS

How can we thank God enough for you in return for all the joy we have in the presence of our God because of you?
1 Thessalonians 3:9 niv

Think of the people God has placed in your life—your family members, friends, coworkers, and other loved ones. They bring much joy and happiness to your life, don't they? Now contemplate this: What if you'd never met any of them? How different would your life be? These folks are such a gift! God has given them to you as a special present—one you need to remember to thank Him for.

Thank You for the people I get to do life with, God. What wonderful gifts they are to me! Amen.

Day 349

YOUR GREAT REWARD

The LORD recompense thy work, and a full reward be given thee.
RUTH 2:12 KJV

Perhaps you feel unappreciated for the things you do for others—the cooking, cleaning, a late night at the office. Just once a thank-you would be reward enough. Someone does take notice of all you do. Your heavenly Father is watching even when it seems no one notices. He's proud of you and appreciates all you do. You show the love and life of God to those around you. Take heart—God is your exceedingly great reward.

God, may all I do bring you honor and glory—even if it is doing laundry and washing dirty dishes. Amen.

Day 350

SHOUTING FOR JOY

Be glad in the LORD and rejoice, you righteous ones;
and shout for joy, all you who are upright in heart.
PSALM 32:11 NASB

Have you ever been so happy that you just felt like shouting? Ever been so overcome with joy that you wanted to holler your praise from the rooftops for all to hear? Well, what's holding you back? Go for it! Shout for joy! Let the whole world hear your praises to the King of kings!

I choose to be glad in You, Lord. I am not ashamed
of the joy I have found in You, my God!

Day 351

THE WORK OF RIGHTEOUSNESS

The work of righteousness shall be peace; and the effect of righteousness quietness and assurance for ever.
ISAIAH 32:17 KJV

What a comfort it is to know that God has paid the price for all your mistakes and declared you righteous based on the life of His own flawless Son. When the enemy comes to condemn you, the blood of Jesus stands between you and anything the devil accuses you of. Jesus paid the price and God found you righteous—without blame. Rest assured that God is on your side. You've been cleared of any wrongdoing by the highest court. You're right in God's eyes.

I am righteous only through the blood of Jesus.
I am thankful that You are on my side, Lord,
and that You see me through a lens of love.

Day 352

OUR EARTHLY LEADERS

The king shall joy in thy strength, O Lord; and
in thy salvation how greatly shall he rejoice!
PSALM 21:1 KJV

Praying for our elected officials is important. They need our undergirding, our daily intercession, and our prayers for their safety and wisdom. Today, as you contemplate your current government leaders, pause a minute and lift their names up in prayer. May they all find strength in the joy of the Lord. May each come to the fullness of salvation. And may the people rejoice as a result of what the Lord has done!

God, bless our leaders. May they know You as
Savior. May they follow hard after You, I pray.

Day 353

BEING ON THE RIGHT PATH

The path of the righteous is like the morning sun,
shining ever brighter till the full light of day.
PROVERBS 4:18 NIV

God knows where you're going. As you journey on the road toward God's purpose and plan for your life, the light of God's love grows brighter with each step, bringing you closer and closer to Him. The more you know Him, the more quickly you know His will and His ways and can more assuredly step out in faith toward His righteous cause. Your steps are sure because your path is well lit with the goodness of God. You're on the right path.

Reveal to me, holy God, step by step, moment by moment,
Your perfect will for me. I will follow You. Amen.

Day 354

SEEDS IN FERTILE SOIL

Light-seeds are planted in the souls of God's people,
joy-seeds are planted in good heart-soil.
PSALM 97:11 MSG

Imagine a farmer dropping seeds into fertile soil. They're sure to spring up. That's how it is with joy. Keep it with you at all times, like seeds in your pocket. Then, when you find fertile soil—in the workplace, at the doctor's office, around the dinner table—pull out a few of those seeds and sprinkle them around. Oh, the joy that will spring forth!

Make me ever mindful of Your light, heavenly Father.
May I share Your joy with the world around me.

Day 355

GIVING UP YOUR BROKENNESS

The sacrifices of God are a broken spirit; a broken
and contrite heart, O God, you will not despise.
PSALM 51:17 ESV

No matter where you've been, God loves you. He doesn't care about your past, but instead wants to give you an awesome future. You were worth the ultimate sacrifice. God gave all He had for you—at the highest cost. He cherishes you more than anything. You are the valuable prize that His Son, Jesus, was willing to fight and die for in order to restore you to your heavenly Father. Give Him your brokenness. It's a sacrifice you can afford to make.

I come humbly before Your throne, Lord. Use this broken
vessel, I ask in Jesus' name. I am at Your service, my King.

Day 356

JOYFUL NOISE, NOT FUSSY COMPLAINTS

Sing for joy to God our strength;
shout aloud to the God of Jacob!
PSALM 81:1 NIV

Imagine you're in a room filled with noisy, fussy, crying children. The combination of their voices raised in miserable chorus is overwhelming. Now imagine that same group of children singing praise to God in unison. They're making a joyful noise— and what a pleasant sound it is! Today, as you face life's many challenges, focus on being a praise giver, not a fussy child.

When I start to whine or complain, change my negative
to positive, Lord. May I praise You in the day-to-day.
May my voice be heard worshipping my King!

Day 357

THE PROMISE
OF THE CROSS

*[God] says, "In the time of my favor I heard you, and in
the day of salvation I helped you." I tell you, now is
the time of God's favor, now is the day of salvation.*
2 Corinthians 6:2 niv

Jesus' death on the cross was God's plan to bring you into heaven
once your time on earth is through. But God had much more in
mind than you might imagine. Jesus' death, burial, and resurrection offer freedom from any bondage you face. God doesn't
want you to miss a single blessing. Let Him save you from worry,
addiction, debt, sickness, and emotional pain. Every promise in
the Book belongs to you. Don't wait to receive His great salvation.

*I receive salvation, and I choose to live the abundant life
now. I won't wait for heaven to begin taking advantage
of all the benefits of being Your child, God!*

Day 358

A LIVING CHURCH

And there was great joy in that city.
ACTS 8:8 NKJV

Can you imagine the church of Jesus Christ—alive and vibrant in every city around the world? Alive in Moscow. Alive in Paris. Alive in Havana. Alive—in your hometown. Oh, the celebration that would ensue if cities around the world were eternally changed. Today, choose a particular city and commit to pray for that place that all might come to know Christ!

Lord, I lift up _____ (name of the city) to You this day. I pray earnestly over all its citizens. No matter how bleak it may seem, I know that in Your power, You can change the hearts of people. May the men and women of this city be saved!

Day 359

MAKING HIS
DEEDS KNOWN

*Give thanks unto the Lord, call upon his name,
make known his deeds among the people.*
1 Chronicles 16:8 kjv

It's one thing to thank God in the privacy of your prayer closet;
it's another to openly talk about the amazing things He has
done in your life in front of a watching world. The words of
your mouth, lifted up in joyful testimony, could have an amazing impact on those around you. So go ahead and thank God
publicly. Share the things He has done with people you come
in contact with. Make His deeds known!

*I will testify of Your goodness, Lord! I will make known the
faithfulness of my God to anyone who will listen. Amen.*

Day 360

WAIT ON THE LORD

Strengthened with all might, according to his glorious power, unto all patience and longsuffering with joyfulness.
COLOSSIANS 1:11 KJV

You've heard the old adage "Don't pray for patience! God will surely give you a reason to need it!" Here's the truth: As you wait on the Lord, He promises to strengthen you with all might, according to His glorious power. So what's a little waiting, as long as God is giving you strength? And you know where that strength comes from after all—the joy of the Lord is your strength!

Waiting is a struggle for me, Father. Make me patient as I wait on You. In Jesus' name, amen.

Day 361

PRESS ON

"I will refresh the weary and satisfy the faint."
JEREMIAH 31:25 NIV

Satisfaction is the result of a job well done. Sometimes your expectation for the blessings of God requires you to press a little harder and stretch your faith a little further to see the results you've asked God for. You can be sure all your effort will be rewarded. God promises to satisfy your soul—a deep satisfaction that only He can provide. He has given you the power to reach your destiny. He will not let you fail. Press on! Press on!

Like a cool drink of water on a hot day is Your Word to my soul, Lord. I will press on toward the prize that awaits me in Christ.

Day 362

TALKING WITH GOD

Let the saints be joyful in glory:
let them sing aloud upon their beds.
Psalm 149:5 kjv

When do you like to spend time alone with the Lord? In the morning, as the stillness of the day sweeps over you? At night, when you rest your head upon the pillow? Start your conversation with praise. Let your favorite worship song or hymn pour forth! Tell Him how blessed you are to be His child. This private praise time will strengthen you and will fill your heart with joy!

I will praise You in the still moments at the beginning and end of my day. You are my God. I will declare Your goodness.

Day 363

GOD IS YOUR SANCTUARY

The righteous will never be moved. . . .
Their hearts are firm, secure in the LORD.
PSALM 112:6–7 NRSV

God is your safe haven from all of life's difficulty. When the pressures of life seem more than you can take, grab hold of the stability found only in Him. You're His for safekeeping. He stands ready to receive you with open arms. The blanket of His love and compassion are there to surround you and bring warmth to your heart during life's coldest hours. Stand under His umbrella of protection throughout the storms. Take refuge in Him—He is your sanctuary!

Keep my eyes fixed on Jesus, I ask You, O God.
May my heart be deeply rooted in Your security. Amen.

Day 364

TRIUMPHING IN CHRIST

*I am grateful that God always makes it
possible for Christ to lead us to victory.*
2 CORINTHIANS 2:14 CEV

God has created us to be victors not victims. We are image bearers of Christ and were born to triumph! So how do you see yourself today? Have you made up your mind to overcome in the areas where you've struggled? One way to assure your victory is to praise God for it even before it happens. That's right! Praise your way through! Oh, the joy of triumphing in Christ!

*I am not a victim but an overcomer through You, Christ Jesus.
I will praise my way through the trials to victory in You! Amen.*

Day 365

THE PERFECT
WORK OF PATIENCE

But let patience have its perfect work, that you
may be perfect and complete, lacking nothing.
JAMES 1:4 NKJV

Let patience have its perfect work? Ouch! It's hard enough to wait, even harder to wait patiently. Now we're supposed to let patience "work" in us while we're waiting? Sounds painful—and nearly impossible! But when we allow patience to have its perfect work in us, we are "complete," wanting nothing. We can wait patiently and not stress about yet unanswered prayers. Every need is met in Christ. Talk about joy!

Patience is a virtue, Lord, but it is not my strong suit. Teach
me to wait quietly before You as You reveal Yourself to me
day by day, hour by hour, moment by moment. Amen.

SCRIPTURE INDEX